To Karren

The good thing about The God
that I know, is that you can be
yourself. Listen (tune in to him)
and he will respond.

Nice meeting you girl.

(Ps. 34)

Sasha
X

Broken, but I'm Healed!

'My journey from heartbreaking pain
to total freedom!'

Sasha D. Taylor

authorHOUSE®

AuthorHouse™ UK Ltd.
500 Avebury Boulevard
Central Milton Keynes, MK9 2BE
www.authorhouse.co.uk
Phone: 08001974150

First published by AuthorHouse 6/16/2009

ISBN: 978-1-4389-7191-9 (sc)

This book is printed on acid-free paper.

"Opening Prayer"

"My Alpha and Omega" – Revelation 21:6

First and foremost, I would like to thank You the Most High God for everything — the good and bad, intended and unintended, planned and unplanned — which you have allowed me to experience over the years. I now know that You were with me every step of the way, preparing me for a time when I would personally testify of Your goodness and mercy to those who call on the name of Jesus in their times of trouble and need. Never in my wildest dreams would I have imagined that You could use my life's experiences, my mess, as an example to help deliver others out of their despair.

I totally believe that my life's experiences have helped to shape and mould me into the person that I am today, uniquely and wonderfully made. And I trust that You will continue to guide, instruct, perfect, and mould me, so that I may become refined like pure gold. I also trust and thank You that You will continue to deliver me out of all the evil works and plans of the enemy *(see Psalm 34:19)*.

Father, let this not be a book about me, but about the greatness of Your mighty power to embrace, to love, to heal, to restore, to change and to deliver those who call upon the name of Jesus *(see Romans 10:8-10)*. Lord, I ask that You use me in any way You choose, so that others may learn from my personal experiences and be healed of the effects of bad relationships that have left so many women broken-hearted.

My Lord God, I know that it is Your desire and will to deliver and set free all oppressed women out of their unfortunate situations and into the abundant life *(John 10:10)*, which You sent Your Son Jesus Christ to give them. For this reason I yield myself completely to Your perfect will and ask that You use me for Your glory.

For everything comes from him and exists by his power and is intended for his glory to him forever! Amen.

Romans 11:36 *(NLT)*

Dedication

I want to dedicate this book to my one and only beautiful son. When the Lord entrusted you to me, I did not know or even comprehend what a blessing you would be to me and my life, but you truly are, son!

In some of my darkest moments it was the thought of you that helped me through. You probably don't remember this, but it was your unique nature as a young child that kept me on the straight and narrow and prevented me from making a lot of mistakes that I would probably regret today.

I regret many things that I have done in my life, son, but you — I could not imagine my life without you in it. Unknowingly, you have taught me how to love someone else unconditionally, and I want you to know that there is nothing that you can ever do that will stop me from loving you.

Despite all that I have put you through, you have still grown up to be a beautiful young man. Even when I shared with you what this book was going to be about you still gave me your blessing and supported me throughout the process of putting it together.

Son, I thank you for the time, encouragement, patience and sacrifice that you gave me while I was writing this book, and I know that the Lord will truly reward you for it. My prayer and desire is that you too will accomplish and fulfil the Lord's plan and purpose for your life.

One last thing Keykey — keep believing in the Lord with all your heart and He will surely give you the desires of your heart. I love you and I will always love you.

All my love, your one and only Mum xxx

Acknowledgements

My Lord and Saviour Jesus Christ — I don't know where I would be if not for your unconditional love! I truly thank you from the bottom of my heart!

"I would like to honour my mother." Mum, I would like to thank you for the times that you struggled through with us. Life was not always easy, but you tried your best to give us what you could. You are a strong woman with a good heart, and I pray that you will learn to believe in yourself much more than you already do. If I could encourage you in one thing, it would be to trust more in the Lord. Mum, I hope one day I will be in a position to grant you that dream of yours, to be 'in the sun.' God knows you deserve it!

Everyone needs someone, a God-sent someone that can see you through when life's cares can get you down. I needed that someone when I could not stand alone and I found it in you, Lorna. You will never really know how much you helped me as I went through my 'fire.' Your prayers, your talks, your love, your encouragement, and your time truly blessed me. You are definitely one of those people that can ask anything of me and I will oblige you because I love you. I guess we are both on our way to fulfilling God's purpose for our lives. See you at the top girl!

To my family, each and every one of you, I pray that you all will experience the magnificent love of God like I have. I love you all so much and I thank the Lord for the fact that I was born into this family. Aunty Dorothy, you in particular have been a rock in this family and are without a doubt my favourite aunty. I thank you for all the love that you have shown me over the years and you too are certainly one of those people who can ask anything of me.

Mum C, I would like to thank you for introducing me to the Lord Jesus

Christ. Even when I did not see a need for Him in my life, you knew that this would be best for me, and you were right. "The Lord does give me a peace that no other person will ever be able to give me." I thank you for all those prayers, and boy, did you say some prayers for me. I do not think I have ever personally met a woman who knows how to show as much love as you do. You will always be dear to my heart.

I would also like to thank each and every one of my friends for the special, unique qualities that you possess and for always being there for me. There were many times when I did not let you know what I was going through because I did not want to worry you, but in your own ways you were all there for me. Thank you, I love you, and trust me when I say that I will not forget you as I embark on my journey with the Lord.

Pastor Clem and Marjorie Esomowei (Triumphant Church International, England), I thank you immensely for being my spiritual parents and guiding me to my purpose. You truly have taught me how to be a warrior for Christ. Pastor Marjorie, I will never forget the shock I received when the Holy Spirit first told me you would assist me in the writing of this book. At first I thought, "Oh no Lord, why Pastor Marjorie? She's so hard working…she is going to make me accountable." But the more time I spent with you Pastor Marjorie the more I warmed to the idea. I have enjoyed every moment we have spent together. I really do thank you Pastor Marjorie for your expertise and the time you invested in me. I love you both.

Sis Eileen, I have not seen you again since that day in 1995 when you declared that the Lord wanted you to anoint my hands because one day I would write books for Him. You do not know this, but at the time I did not believe a word of that prayer, and in my heart I laughed my head off and thought you were crazy. *Write books for the Lord*, I thought to myself, *this woman can't be hearing from the Lord*. Well, one of the books that you anointed my hands to write is now completed. Sister Eileen, I want to first apologise to you for my impoliteness, and then I would like to thank you for your obedience, because you were right!

I could not end this section without giving my thanks and appreciation to all the music ministers that have unknowingly helped to minister the Lord's healing and deliverance power to me over the years. If it wasn't for the ministry of music, I do not know how I would have survived those lonely and trying times! So I thank you all from the bottom of my heart. And to one in particular — there is just something about your voice, gift and humbleness that enables me to enter into the Lord's presence so smoothly. Stay in His presence girl, because you truly bless me!

Contents

Introduction

On the surface everything in my life seemed to be going great. I had accepted the Lord as my Saviour. I had a loving boyfriend and a beautiful son, and to top it off I had started to focus my attentions and actions towards mapping out an honest career for myself. Things could not have been any better!

So why then was my soul not feeling happy or satisfied with all of these things that I already had? What more could I have possibly wanted or needed to make myself feel happier and content?

I accepted the Lord as my Saviour a few years before I had come to this point of discontent, but I had not been serious about developing my relationship with Him. My loving boyfriend, who I had grown up with since I was a teenager, did not seem to have the qualities that I wanted in a man. My young son's dependency on me was beginning to worry me, and although I had started a vocational college course, I was not sure whether I had the ability to complete it. So to an outsider looking in it may have seemed like everything was going great, but to me, deep down on the inside, I could not escape the feeling that something was still missing from my life, something I could not quite place my finger on!

My relationship with the Lord was a slow one in the making. It did not start off in the straightforward way that I have heard others describe. Mine was a slow and gradual process. After accepting Jesus Christ as my Lord and Saviour, I still continued to live my life pretty much the same way that I always had before I made this decision. The only difference was now I knew and believed there was a God out there somewhere. During this time I may not have completely believed that this God could possibly help me find answers for my discontent, but I was relatively sure of the fact that He existed. So I was happy to seek Him from time to time to let Him know how I was getting on and tell

Him of any needs that I had. Other than this, my relationship with the Lord was very weak!

In most cases a person's discontent will inevitably lead him or her to take some sort of action or change to rectify the situation. And that's what happened to me. My discontent eventually forced me to make some life-changing decisions. They were changes that I may not have wanted to make, but they were certainly changes that I needed to implement if my relationship with the Lord was to develop and grow. The bottom line was that I urgently needed to put the Lord first in my life above all other things!

It did not occur to me until long afterwards that the emptiness which I was experiencing was a direct result of the fact that I had not sought a more meaningful relationship with my Lord and Saviour *(see John 6:35)*. I had lived my life for years without a Lord or Saviour and things seemed to be going great so to simply hand my life over to the Lord, like I was being advised to, did not come naturally to me. Before I could do this with anyone, I would first have to build up my trust in them, right!

In the meantime, I continued to trust in things that I believed would benefit my life, like the man that I had grown up with, the man that I had loved from a young age, and believed would never hurt me. It had been easy to love this man because over the years he had seemingly proved himself trustworthy to me. But trusting in the Lord Jesus Christ, that was a different story altogether!

If someone had come and announced to me that the man I had trusted with my whole heart would one day leave me so broken-hearted I would even contemplate suicide, I would not have believed them — it just seemed totally impossible to me! The chance of this happening was so unlikely that even if the Lord himself had come down from heaven and told me this was about to happen, I would not have believed Him. *Anyway, how could he break my heart? What did a broken heart even feel like? Could I possibly love this man that much? Surely I am in control of things and this could not happen to me?* (These questions would probably have been my response to a prediction of this kind.)

2

Well, as you can guess, that day did come and I was left so broken-hearted by it all that I even contemplated suicide. The whole experience came about so unexpectedly that it knocked the life out of me, and the shock and pain of it all was so horrific!

I am pretty sure that most of us have been horribly shocked at one time or another in our lives, so you will probably be familiar with some of the feelings that can follow such an experience, such as panic, denial, numbness, pain, hurt, unbelief, confusion, blame, and anger. Well, I experienced all of these feelings to some degree or another and it was painful!

In my desperate attempt to free myself from the pain of my broken heart, I finally turned, confused and desperate, to the Lord for help. I did not expect Him to answer me because of the way that I had treated Him beforehand, but to my surprise He did! Not only did the Lord hear my cry for help, He rescued me. He delivered me, He cleaned me up, He healed me, He restored my heart and soul and placed my feet upon the rock! *(See Psalm 27:5.)*

The Holy Spirit once told me that "my testimony would never be really effective and help to set others free if I did not share the fullness of it with them." Although it's been almost six years since the end of this whole episode and from that exact moment when the Holy Spirit first spoke this to me, these words still stand out to me as clearly as if they were only spoken yesterday.

At the time when the Holy Spirit first told me this, I did not really know why He had said it or what was in store for me, but as I sit here pondering what these words actually mean to me now, I realise that it was the Lord's intention for me to share the fullness of my story with others. The Lord already knew back in 2003 that one day in my future, I would come to a place of trust in Him where I would agree to write this book in the way that He had intended for it to be written. The truth is I was destined to write this book!

In the book of Revelation, Chapter 12 verse 11 it says, *"And they have defeated him by the blood of the Lamb and by their testimony. And they did not love their lives so much that they were afraid to die"* (NLT). So when the Holy Spirit asked me to write this book in order to help others overcome their pain, I knew in my heart that if I obeyed Him and shared it all in the way that it really happened, the Lord would then be able to use me to pull down the devil's stronghold and power over the lives of many. And it is for this reason that I have agreed to tell you it all — every painful and embarrassing detail that I personally experienced.

". . . Remember that your Christian brothers and sisters all over the world are going through the same suffering you are. . ." 1 Peter 5:9 (NLT).

Before I became familiar with this Scripture, I thought I was the only person in the world that had experienced a seriously broken heart. I believed that I was on my own in this situation and as a result of this, I originally vowed to keep this painful experience to myself for the rest of my life. However, the truth is that I am not alone. Many have been through my experience, many are still going through it, and many will soon go through it!

I honestly do believe that there are a lot of genuine people out there that would really appreciate help to overcome similar situations and it is for this reason that I have agreed to share my story.

I titled this book *Broken, but I'm Healed!* after hearing a song with the same title by Byron Cage. As I sat listening to the words of that song on his MySpace site it suddenly dawned on me that the words of this song actually summed up everything that I wished to say to all who read this book. (I encourage you to go and listen to that song because it will truly bless you.)

I may have been through the floods and the fire, but I want you all to know that the Lord has been faithful to me, and has totally delivered and healed me of my broken heart. He has also proved to me that He is faithful to His Word; and I believe that He can do the same in your life!

The only thing that you will have to do is let go — let go of all those other things that you are trusting in for your help. I challenge you to *breakthrough and trust and obey the Lord God Almighty!*

As you read through my story, my pain, my hurt, my struggles, my misery, my distress, my deliverance, my healing, and my victory, I want you to know that the Lord has brought me safely through to my expected end *(see Jeremiah 29:11)* — *My heart was once broken, but now I am Healed!*

"My Prayer for You"

I pray that this book, inspired, ordained, and commissioned by the Holy Spirit, will touch and set free all women who for one reason or another have been left broken-hearted as a result of an unhealthy relationship.

I pray that the Lord will give me the wisdom, boldness, and courage which surpasses all understanding to open up and share my heart and personal experiences freely with you all, as God so freely shared His Son Jesus Christ with us *(see John 3:16-17).*

My prayer for you is that through the help and guidance of the Holy Spirit you will also find hope, deliverance, healing, and restoration in the Lord, and know that He has a plan and purpose for your future in Him. I also pray that like me, you also may overcome the things sent to abort the plan and purpose of God for your life.

And finally, my prayer for you is that once the Lord has finished carrying out His miraculous healing and restoration in your life, you too will obtain the courage through God's Word and the guidance of the Holy Spirit to go out into the world and win souls for the kingdom of God with your own testimonies.

For the Word of God says, "they overcame him (devil) by the blood of the Lamb, and by the word of their testimony." Revelations 12:11 (KJV)

Amen

Chapter One

Through it all!

Let me introduce myself - Exodus 3:14

Before I begin sharing my personal experiences with you regarding the subject of my broken heart, I would like to first share with you a bit about who I am and where I am at in this stage of my life. I have decided to do this so that you will know that although I was once in a terrible way, the Lord totally delivered me and healed my broken heart.

It does not make any difference who you are, where you come from, or even your status in life. Let's face it, a broken heart is simply a broken heart and it can affect anyone! So although it may not seem like I come from the same walk of life as you, I would like you to simply pray and ask the Holy Spirit why He wants you to read this book. And I would like you to allow Him to speak to you through these words as you read them with an expectant heart. I believe that you have not simply come across this book by accident, but that it is by God's perfect will and divine appointment that He has connected you to me (*see Psalms 32:8*).

I still sometimes find it hard to comprehend how the Lord was able to bring me out of my despair, but I rejoice in the fact that He did. I also rejoice in the fact that as a result of you choosing to read this book, the Lord's intention and desire is to do it for you also. If you fully co-operate and allow Him to carry out the work necessary on your behalf, you too will be well on your way to recovery and restoration.

The Lord transformed me from a girl without any real plan or purpose — a girl who used to do almost nothing and expect to get everything back in return — into a woman with a plan and purpose and a new passion for life.

I really do thank the Lord for the day that I accepted His Way and made the decision to follow Him. Since then He has led me through so many challenges. Some I have enjoyed, some have stretched me, and there have even been some that I have shied away from. But one thing I can say about the Lord is that He has always brought me through them all *(see Psalm 23).*

I would describe myself as a normal thirty-something-year-old, mother of one. I live with my son and generally we get along well together. At the moment I do not have that 'perfect' life partner, but I am prepared to wait for him, as I trust the Lord to connect us together at the appointed time *(see Habakkuk 2:3).* In the meantime I have decided to continue to develop an intimate relationship with my Lord and Saviour and make Him my example and focus. I am at present a nursery school teacher and I enjoy my job. I have a supportive extended family that I see regularly, and financially I am sufficiently comfortable for this stage of my life, although I do believe that my best is yet to come! Overall, I would say that my life is going pretty well at the moment.

However, I do not credit my current success to any of the reasons that I have just previously mentioned. Instead, I would say that my decision to make the Lord a major part of my life was—and still is—the key to my successes. In all essence I have given my life over to the Lord to help me to live a more abundant life. And He has certainly proven to me that He can do a much better job with it than I ever could. It took me awhile to surrender all to the Lord, and occasionally He still has to remind me who is in charge. But I now have a special relationship with Him and I have learned to trust Him in a way that I have never trusted anyone else before.

My decision to surrender all and hand my life over to the Lord was not an easy one, and there were times when I struggled tremendously with the concept of doing so. As a matter of fact, I wrestled on and off with the Lord for years, like Jacob did with the man in the book of Genesis,

Chapter 32. And like Jacob, I too became so tired and weak of trying to do things my way that I had no other choice but to give up my fight and surrender all.

I first gave my life to the Lord about fourteen years ago, and during this time I have taken it back a number of times: I had my son out of wedlock, wilfully disobeyed God's known will stated in the Bible, ignored the Holy Spirit's leadings, acted in a way that did not glorify Him, got angry with Him, murmured against Him, questioned His ability to rule, and continued for years to have sex with a man that I was not married to. My lists of imperfections were endless, and I would never claim otherwise. The truth is that I continued to do all the things that I knew the Lord disliked and this rarely bothered me. So as you can see I am not 'perfect,' and I would never claim to be!

Although I was hopelessly struggling with these issues of sin, I was quite wise in the sense that I did not try to conceal my sins from the Lord, and I would constantly bring them before Him and ask for help in overcoming them. I was not stupid enough to think or believe that the Lord could not see what I was doing, so for this reason I would consistently confess my sins and ask the Lord to help me to turn away from them and help me live in the way that would glorify Him.

Proverbs 28:13 says, *"People who conceal their sins will not prosper, but if they confess and turn away from them they will receive mercy"* (NLT).

It may have taken me a lot longer than others to get myself in line with God's will and direction for my life, but the lessons I learned during this period will never be forgotten. I believe that they have given me the wisdom I need to help others overcome similar life challenges.

Don't get me wrong, I am not trying to say that it is acceptable to continue committing sin while simply confessing it, as this is most definitely not an attitude that I want to promote. I am just letting you know the place where I was at in my own life. The main reason I chose to confess my sins to the Lord was purely because I did not want or wish to continue down the path to despair and destruction I was on.

Proverbs 16:6, Amplified version reads, *"by mercy and love, truth and fidelity [to God and man-not by sacrificial offerings], iniquity is purged out of the heart, and by the reverent, worshipful fear of the Lord men depart from and avoid evil."*

In my heart I really did want to stop many of the things I was doing because apart from the fact that the Word of God tells us *(Romans 6:23)* that "the wages of sin is death," I was becoming more and more conscious of how the Lord was viewing me and how I was letting Him and myself down by continuously disobeying His Word *(see Romans 6)*.

A hard lesson - Psalm 34:19

My purpose for writing this book is to testify and share with you how the Lord came and healed my broken heart at a time when it had been left so badly wounded as the result of a relationship that went terribly wrong. So let me begin.

The relationship that broke my heart was my first real relationship with a man — in fact, he was my 'first love.' It was a relationship that I entered into blinded by lust and love because I had no other experiences to compare it with. I was totally opened to all the risks that you take when you do things out of God's perfect will and as a result I suffered tremendously for it. I did not guard my heart *(Proverbs 4:23)* like I was supposed to because at the time I did not realise that I could literally die from the pain of a broken heart. I was young, naïve, immature, and easily impressed at the time of this relationship. And I certainly did not have a clue about what I was getting myself into — I thought it would last forever!

My broken heart was quite severe, severe enough for me to contemplate suicide a number of times. It lasted for a number of years, about five to be precise, not because the Lord was not on time to save me but because I kept going back to the things that He was constantly telling me to turn away from, such as continuing to have sex with this man, even when I knew he had started a new relationship with somebody else.

My sexual sin played a big part in the unnecessary length of time it took for the Lord to deliver me out of my despair. I totally accept that it was my fault and my lack of strength to make a decision to turn away from this area of sin that kept me in bondage for so long.

As you read on, I will address this issue further and explain to you why I have come to this conclusion. I will also show how you can receive your deliverance and healing a lot quicker than I did simply by being obedient to the known will of God.

The blessings in the storm - Luke 8:22-25

During this dark period of my life I would like to point out that there was also a positive side which I knew to be blessings from God. I had my young son who I love and adore, my college course, and then a university course, and my family and friends that loved me. But above all of that, I had decided to seek after a more meaningful relationship with the Lord!

My decision to give the Lord a chance in my life came about mainly because I knew that I had no other choice or place to turn. I had already tried everything else that I knew to do and nothing seemed to work. (Isn't it funny how most people seem to make God their last option after all else fails and they can't seem to see their way out of a bad situation? Yet, the real truth is that we all need the Lord at all times, even when things are going well!)

Before I go on, I want to tell you today that God is not put off at all by this human trait and that He loves us and desires to be in continuous fellowship with us all the time. To really understand this concept you just have to look at the way we treated God's Son Jesus when He sent him to redeem us. We crucified him for absolutely nothing, but God still loved us and wanted us reconciled to Him. Another good thing I would like to share with you is that Lord does not force Himself upon anyone. He is what I would call a gentleman! He simply waits until we are ready and then He reveals Himself to us. What I am trying to say could not be explained better than in Romans 1:6 in the Amplified Bible, which says: *"and this included you, called of Jesus Christ and invited [as you are} to belong to him."*

It was the things I viewed as positive that kept me going during this dark period, and to be honest with you, I do not know how I got through it but by God's grace, mercy, and help. Can you imagine waking up with a broken heart every single day for years, pretending to be alright to the outside world, attending college and university, meeting deadlines, juggling a young son's needs and then going to bed with your same old broken heart day after day, and night after night? And did I mention the constant torment waged against my mind every waking moment? Or, the voices that would constantly tell me, "You cannot make it!" "You will never make it!" "You can't possibly go on!" And, "Why don't you just give up?"

In the beginning stages of my distress, it was my son that gave me the strength and will to carry on, because I couldn't help but wonder what would happen to him if I decided to take my own life.

At this point I would like to stress that committing suicide is not the answer to your problems. Aside from the fact that other loved ones are left deeply devastated by such actions, it is not God's will for anyone to take his or her life. In John 10:10, Jesus, "our ultimate head Shepherd," warns us that the devil comes to steal from us, and to try to kill and destroy us. But we should not stop reading there because Jesus then goes on to tell us that the purpose for His coming was to give us an abundant life. I like how it reads in the Amplified version of the Bible: *"The thief comes only in order to steal and kill and destroy. I came that they may have and enjoy life, and have it in abundance (to the full, till it overflows)."*

Yes, it is true that I did get close to the point of giving up my will to live, but knowing that my son depended on me for almost everything kept me waking up each morning and carrying on in my pain.

The fact that the Lord was now my source of encouragement and help enabled me to face each day as it came. And the fact that I had decided to carry on for my son's sake meant that I would have to find a way to get up and start living again. I mean, I could not go on any longer in my pain, it was unbearable.

So after trying almost every other avenue that I knew, I turned to the Lord. And what can I say, He picked me up, He restored me, He embraced me, He loved me, He cared for me, He held me, He delivered me, He gave me the strength, power, and authority to change my situation. . . *He healed my broken heart!*

The Lord reveals His plans to me - Ephesians 3:6

On Wednesday, February 21ˢᵗ, 2001, I was at home alone watching a Christian video that I had borrowed from a good friend. T.D. Jakes was the speaker and the message he was preaching was based on the story of Moses questioning God's decision to use him for the great task of leading the Israelites into the Promised Land *(see Exodus 3 & 4)*. The message preached was called "A Stick and A Stutter" and T.D. Jakes was re-enacting the scene where God was preparing Moses to lead His people to the Promised Land. "It is not you (Moses), it is Me, and it's My anointing!" T.D. Jakes shouted, referring to God trying to get Moses to see beyond his own abilities to His supernatural empowerment.

As T.D. Jakes, in his great style of bringing Biblical stories to life, echoed the words, "It's not you, it's Me," his words began to ring out in my spirit and the manifested power of God came down on me, right there in my living room. The whole atmosphere changed in an instant and it was as if God was personally speaking these words to me.

When I say the "power of God came down" I can only explain it as a feeling of being in the presence of a greater being than myself. It was an overpowering presence that made me physically weak and almost unable to move. It is hard to explain such a personal experience to someone else, and unless you have actually had a similar experience with the Lord, it may be a little hard to comprehend what I am saying. So for argument sake, let's just say that I knew that the Spirit of God was present with me in my living room that night.

As I sat there shaking and weak under the power of God, I began to hear Isaiah 61:1 over and over again in my spirit: *"The Spirit of the Lord is upon me: because the Lord hath anointed me to preach good tidings unto the meek; he hath sent me to bind up the broken-hearted, to proclaim liberty to the captives, and the opening of the prison to them that are bound."* I was familiar with this verse of Scripture, but I did not know it to recite it in the way that I was hearing it in my spirit, as I was not a great reader of the Bible at this time!

As the realisation of what was happening to me began to sink in, the Holy Spirit began to reveal to me part of His plan for my life. I had asked the Holy Spirit on several occasions before this moment what His plan and purpose was for me but had never before received a clear answer until now.

Everyone around me seemed to know what the Lord's amazing purpose was for their lives, so I badgered the Holy Spirit constantly to reveal to me what my God-given purpose was. I had come to a place where I really needed to know because I was at a point of giving up on life.

The Lord is more than good in so many ways. And one way is that He knows what we need exactly when we need it, and will never let us down! When the Lord first revealed His plans to me in the natural, I was a long way from actually believing that I could ever reach such a position. But the Lord knew that I needed to hear it at that moment in time or else it could have been too late.

After the Holy Spirit had finished ministering to me, I then asked the question, "If this is really your plan for me, why have you allowed me to suffer in pain for so long when you could have easily removed it from me at any time?" The Holy Spirit's response to this was, "Because of your personal experience of this kind of pain, you will now be able to minister with compassion to my broken-hearted women who like you have been left battered and wounded by the effects of an unpleasant relationship or breakup." The Holy Spirit then went on to say that He could now use me as a vessel to help bring His healing power to others with compassion because of my first hand personal experience and understanding of this kind of pain.

After this very personal encounter with the Lord that night I remember I cried and cried for ages. It was a cry of pain, relief, doubt, unbelief, and confusion, all wrapped up into one. I also remember asking the Holy Spirit over and over again, "How could He possibly use me to do such a great task?" Because apart from anything else at that particular moment, all I could think about was myself and whether or not I would ever get over my own broken heart. At a time when I was still questioning the Lord's ability and power to heal me of my constant torment and broken heart, it was hard to comprehend that one day the Lord would use me to help others to get over theirs.

Despite all the future challenges that I still had to face and overcome, this divine revelation from the Lord gave me new hope. I started to feel like I could actually carry on with my life because the Lord God Almighty actually had something important for me to do for Him — 'a special job' — that only I could perform!

That night I remember feeling so loved and important. But like everything worthwhile, this revelation was only part of the process and I still had a long way to go on my journey to freedom!

An extra-ordinary meeting – Matthew 19:26

In February 2003, I was invited to a church meeting by a good friend of mine. I had attended many small gatherings during this period of my life but none had ever compared to this one. This meeting was not an ordinary meeting by far! It was a meeting with a bit of a difference, and as you read on you will see why.

Before I went to the meeting I was aware that some of my ex-boyfriend's family members would be there. So I prepared for this by putting on my usual 'got it all together' mask to disguise my hurt and pain. It all seemed like it was going to be a straightforward process. My plan was to attend, listen to the speaker, endure, and then leave. But there was one problem — I did not know that my ex's current partner was going to be there too!

I do not remember if I got there before her or after her — honestly, I could not tell you that for this information seems like a thing of the past — like those things of little relevance or importance that you just can't remember. However, ask me how I felt and I can give you this information with great detail. I was angry! I was angry at the fact that I had been put in this situation . . . yet again, and that I had allowed myself to be put there.

Prior to attending this meeting, I had been feeling a little deflated because of some life-changing situations going on around me. I came to this meeting with the mindset that I would come only because my good friend had invited me and not because I really wanted to be there. I would listen to the speaker, then go home and continue trying to sort out my life. So at the sight of my ex's girlfriend, I kept telling myself, *I knew I should not have come here* . . . To sum it up in one word, I was fuming! Of course I did not let this show outwardly, but God knew I was furious. I kept this to myself and tried my best not to let it show to anyone because after almost three years, even I was getting fed up with the fact that I could not seem to get over this man.

I remember sitting at the back of the hall trying my best to fully focus on the speaker's touching life story about the terrible despair the Lord had delivered her from. From time to time I'd say a little prayer under my breath and ask the Holy Spirit to give me the strength to endure this awkward situation. And as always before, the Lord gave me the strength I needed.

For the past few years this girl had been my No. 1 enemy, not literally, but in my mind (*see Romans 8:6, AMP*). This was someone that I had not really known, but I hated her with all my being because of what I felt she had done to me.

16

Looking back on the experience I cannot help but feel silly and a bit embarrassed about the way I acted towards her. But the good news is that I have moved on from that era of my life and I totally accept that my judgment and treatment of this person were totally unjustified.

At this moment of writing, a saying that I have often heard over the years comes to mind. I am not quite sure where it comes from or who first said it, but it goes like this: "Hurting people usually hurt others!" This is the only way I can explain my attitude, thoughts, and actions towards her, and I thank God that I have matured and grown up since then.

If I was to say that this meeting was a little awkward it would be an understatement, and if it was not for the realness and openness of the speaker's testimony, I probably would have gotten up and left.

The woman of God gave a very explicit testimony about where she had been when the Lord delivered her. She had previously been a prostitute for a number of years until the Lord had intervened, fixed up her life, and was now using her to tell others that He wanted to do the same for them too.

As she shared some very personal details with us, I sat there in awe of her, asking myself, *how does someone get to that place where they will share all of this for the Lord?* I also remembered thinking to myself, *Thank you Lord that no one will ever have to know about the great pain and distress that I went through. Surely, Lord, you would not expect me to be as open as that when it is time to tell my story!* And it was at that moment, right there in that meeting when I decided that if the Lord ever permitted me to share my testimony in order to minister to others, I would keep it short and sweet and leave out all the most painful and embarrassing details. The reason why I made this conscious decision was because a lot of the things I was experiencing were still hurting me and I was extremely embarrassed by the fact that I had let myself slip to such an all-time low.

What's going on Lord? – Isaiah 55:8

Towards the end of the woman's testimony about her remarkable life story, the Holy Spirit intervened and used her to speak directly to a few people in the audience. One of them was my ex-partner's girlfriend. I could not tell you word for word what was said because at the time I was too busy questioning God about his reasons for doing such a private thing at this appointed time, but the words that were spoken were along the lines of this: "The man that you chose for yourself was not My choice or My will for you . . . I will restore you, heal you, and give you the man that I have chosen for you."

I cannot speak for anyone else in that meeting because I do not know what was going through their minds at that point, but I can speak for myself and tell you exactly what went through my mind.

My mind quickly tuned to the matter at hand and went through a number of thoughts and feelings in the space of a few minutes, and I will share a few with you. My first thought was that I could not help feeling that the Lord was on my side and showing me favour in this situation. Let me explain this feeling in order to give you some understanding of what I mean.

For the past few years I had been compared to this girl not only by my ex-partner but by some members of his family and also by me. Outwardly she seemed to have all the godly qualities that I did not seem to have. She was kind, sweet, very humble, caring, and would always put herself out for others.

You may be asking yourself how I could have known all of this about her if I did not really know her. Well, it's simple. Apart from the fact that I would often find myself comparing myself to her, the devil also seized the opportunity to rub salt in my wounds by encouraging others to share such information with me. The devil is not stupid! He knows exactly what your weaknesses are, and he will always use others to tell you things that he knows will hurt and upset you. And the funny thing is, they may not even realise that they are actually hurting you.

When the Lord speaks about man looking at the outward appearance and not the inner heart in 1 Samuel 16:7 He definitely knew what He was talking about. Don't get me wrong, I am not saying that this person had a bad heart or anything like that. I am simply saying that just because a person does not conform to another person's liking or choice of behaviour, does not mean the person does not have a sincere heart. Only God can determine or know the true motives of a person's actions or heart!

My second thought was, *Lord, why have you chosen to do something so private so publicly?* There were a lot of people at that meeting; people that had known the ins and outs of the whole situation, and I could not understand why the Holy Spirit had picked this particular time to reveal something like that to her. (I cannot be 100 percent sure, but I really do believe that the Lord wanted to make His will known to us all.)

And the final thought that I will share with you is my feeling of compassion for this girl. I knew right there and then that her heart was in pain. I knew that she was experiencing some of the same pain I had felt and was still feeling. And in that short moment my attitude towards her changed from one of hatred and resentment to absolute compassion.

"Compassion?" I hear someone ask. "How on earth could you feel compassion towards her?"

Well, I honestly do not really know how I made this transition. All I know is that the pain I had felt in my situation I would not have wished upon my worst enemy. For this reason alone I felt compassion for her.

It was at this point that I knew that the Lord had done something in me because I could not have had this change of heart without His intervention. If you can cast your mind back to that night when the Lord first revealed His plan and purpose for me, you will remember that He told me that the reason He had allowed me to go through so much pain was so I would be able to show this compassion towards other women experiencing such things. What I did not realise or even comprehend at the time was that in just less than two years I would be at this meeting expressing this compassion to the woman involved in breaking my own heart.

I know, it is almost unbelievable that the Lord would set up such a thing — but wait, the story does not end here, look what He does next!

Before the guest speaker began to pray for my ex-partner's girlfriend she stared straight into my eyes and asked, "Can you come and help me pray for this young lady?"

Now you have to remember that this guest speaker is not aware of any connections as she makes this request to me, and it is fair to say that she had not met either of us before this point. This was definitely a God ordained moment.

By now I was fully aware that the presence of the Lord was moving strongly in that meeting and I felt that He was really trying to challenge me. *No way Lord, I can't do that*, was my response for a number of reasons. One reason being, I knew that certain people in the meeting would be baffled by such actions because even I was baffled as to why the Holy Spirit would ask me to do this.

As I wrestled with why I would not go forward and pray for her, the Holy Spirit continued to prompt me to get up out of my seat anyway. There was a part of me that did really want to pray for her because I knew she was going through some pain at this time, but an even bigger part of me did not want to pray for her because in my mind I was still blaming her for the pain I was still going through.

Anyway, one minute I was sitting there debating what I should do and the next minute I was out of my seat and praying alongside a few others for the girl that I once believed helped to break my heart. At first I felt a little awkward and I was more conscious of my surroundings than I was about sincerely praying for her. The Lord was obviously aware of my attitude because as we all stood there praying for her He suddenly allowed me to feel her inner pain.

As I began to experience her pain, my own heart began to ache and feel discomfort and it was as if my heart was being tied up into tight knots. The tears began to roll down my face as I began to identify this feeling with the one I myself had experienced.

"Can you feel it?" the Holy Spirit asked me. "Can you feel her pain?"

"Yes, of course I can," I answered quietly. And the worst thing was that I knew in my heart of hearts that I had contributed to this pain!

Lord, you're not finished yet . . . you mean there's more? – Matthew 5:3-12

After praying for this girl, I remembered feeling a little awkward as I went back to my seat. My friend had organised the meeting and had to wait until the end so she could lock up the hall. So I sat in the background wondering how much longer she would be and waiting anxiously for the meeting to finish up.

As the prayer line came to an end my friend asked if I wanted the guest speaker to pray with me. "No, it's alright," I answered. (The Holy Spirit had done enough for me in this meeting, and to be honest with you I just wanted to go home to my own pity party and chew on things on my own.) I was quite adamant that I did not want any prayers that night, but after some encouragement I finally gave in and went forward to the woman of God for prayer.

Within a moment after joining her, the Holy Spirit began to speak to me through this woman. The words she spoke were not new to me because I had actually heard some of them before. The Holy Spirit used this woman (that I had never met before) to confirm to me the assignment that He had first revealed to me two years earlier in February 2001. I can't remember her exact words, but here is a paraphrase of what this woman of God said to me: "You are misunderstood by people but God sees your heart and He likes it because you have a heart for the Lord. The reason He has allowed you to have experienced so much pain is because you will minister His healing power all over the world to women who have been through and are going through the same pain as you have. God has given you a new name: Sought After. No longer will you be called Misunderstood, and the reason the devil has tried to destroy you so fiercely is because he knows the calling upon your life and your destiny!"

This word of confirmation and encouragement came as a delightful surprise to me because the Holy Spirit had confirmed to me, through someone I had never met, the same revelation that He had given me back in 2001. And to unexpectedly hear these words again was so uplifting and encouraging — it was unbelievable!

Even after hearing it again in these circumstances there was still a part of me that could not fully comprehend what I was hearing. (To be honest with you I had kind of given up on the thought of actually doing any of the things the Lord had said I would do because of the length of time that had passed since He first revealed it to me.) The fact that nothing seemed to be happening in relation to God's plan and purpose for my life had made me partially give up on the idea of it ever happening.

The woman minister concluded her time with me by saying, "You already know what I am saying to you because the Lord has already revealed this to you personally, right?"

I am not going to lie to you. I left that place on cloud nine! "Lord, you mean that you are still going to use me, despite all the disobedience and problems that I continue to cause?"

Boy, I thank God that He looks at the heart of men and not our outer actions or thoughts, or else I would have been doomed!

The anointing destroys the yoke! – Isaiah 10:27

In April 2003, a few months after that "extra-ordinary meeting," I was at the Easter Sunday service at my church when the Holy Spirit suddenly began to speak to me. He told me that He wanted to set me free from some strongholds that were governing my life. I do not mind sharing this with you now, but there was definitely a time when I would not have wanted to share this with you for all sorts of reasons, mainly the shame and embarrassment I felt about the whole thing.

During the service, as the whole congregation was praising and worshiping the Lord, the Holy Spirit gently told me to tell the demonic spirits *(see Matthew17:14-20, Mark 5:1-20, 9:14-32, Luke 8:26-39, 11:14-28)* oppressing me — the ones that I had given authority to reside within me because of my previous lifestyle — that they had to leave me today in Jesus' Name. The Holy Spirit then said to me, "When Pastor Clem invites the people forward for prayer, you must go down and I will set you free."

"What? Excuse me? Lord is that you? I can't do something like that Lord! I'm scared!" These were a few of the thoughts that sprang to my mind. (To be honest with you, at the time I actually doubted that it was really the Holy Spirit speaking to me as this kind of thing had never happened to me before.)

I stood there for a moment in a kind of daze, wondering what was really going on, until I heard something within me start to speak out and discuss with me why it was not a good idea for me to go down to the front to receive prayer and deliverance. The voice even told me what it was going to do to me if I did go forward for prayer.

At first I ignored the Holy Spirit because I could not believe that He would expect me, an inexperienced Christian, to do such a thing on my own, but as He continued to gently speak to me, I soon realised that this was real and happening to me.

I was frozen with fear. My legs began to wobble and the palms of my hands began to sweat profusely. But with all this going on, in all the commotion, just as the Holy Spirit had said to me minutes before, Pastor Clem gave the invitation to come forward for prayer and the calm voice of the Holy Spirit continued to beckon me down. "Come . . . come . . . come!" He kept saying to me. I had almost made up my mind and was just about to go down to the front when I heard a clear demonic voice say to me, "If you go, I am going to kill you!"

I am not going to lie to you, I was absolutely terrified at this moment, but at the sound of this threatening voice, complete boldness came over me and I replied back to it, "You can't kill me or you would have done so already." I do not know how I got down those steps that day, as I was disabled with fear, but I made it. I made up my mind that I was going to be set free and nothing was going to stop me!

While I was standing in the prayer line waiting for my turn, the demonic voice continued to make suggestions to me as to why I should go back to my seat and one of the things that struck me at this point was how scared and defeated the voice had now become in comparison to when it first spoke to me. The more it spoke to me the more I remember crying out to the Lord that I wanted Him to set me free and that I was sorry that I had continued to disobey His Word even when I knew it to be right.

The outcome was just as the Holy Spirit said it would be, and I was set free from what I now know to be spirits of perversion, pride, and bondage.

My deliverance experience was like nothing that had ever happened to me and it really opened my eyes to some spiritual implications concerning my actions. As a young Christian I had witnessed others being set free from demonic oppression countless times but I never believed that anything like that could ever happen to me. In fact, I used to think to myself, *God, what awful things could these people have possibly done to end up being oppressed by a demonic spirit?*

Over that entire Easter weekend the Lord continued to free and cleanse me from demonic oppression on at least three more separate occasions, and it is an experience that I will never forget!

Totally moved with compassion! – Matthew 9:36

In the month of November 2003, I was with a friend of mine, sitting in my car and earnestly trying to convince her that the situation she had gotten herself into was not the will of God for her life. I had not been in exactly the same situation as her but I was familiar with her feeling of wanting to be loved by a man, even if the circumstances were not ideal or according to God's will. So for these reasons alone her situation really touched me! Like her, at that particular moment, the devil had also tried to destroy my life by keeping me entangled in a cycle of sin and a bad relationship so that I could not fully experience the great love of God. And he was trying to use a man in order to do so. However, I was lucky, so to speak, that I had experienced the Lord's salvation some time before my dilemma and was able to use the little knowledge and understanding that I had of the Lord to seek Him in my time of distress.

For years I had struggled with my issue of a broken heart, just like the woman in the Bible with an issue of blood in Luke 8:40-48. And like this woman with the issue of blood, the Lord had been merciful and faithful in delivering me out of my distress and putting me on the road to recovery and victory. It was a process, a long one thanks to my inability to let go, but the Lord really did tarry with me and eventually heal me of my broken heart.

So as I sat there reasoning with my friend about her situation, I could feel a strong desire building up in my heart and soul, a desire to see her free from her unhealthy relationship. I do not really know why I was feeling like this because it was not as if her situation was affecting me in anyway, but for some reason I started to feel a great compassion towards her. On that day I remember going home and thinking to myself, *Lord, why do we beautiful women fall for the same old tricks time and time again when it comes to men and relationships? Why can we not see that it is just a distraction of the enemy to keep us all tied up and unable to reach our destinies? Why do we look for love in all the wrong places, when it is right here in You?*

Don't get me wrong, I totally understand why we women have such issues and go through such things, but after years of reading and studying the Word of God and being in close fellowship with Him really does give you a better perspective of your self-worth as a woman. It also makes you wonder why we would even allow these things to happen to us!

Write down the vision! – Habakkuk 2:2-3

Later on that same evening, I was talking to the Holy Spirit about my desire to see my friend get out of her situation very quickly when the Holy Spirit shared with me that He wanted me to record my testimony concerning my broken heart. I did not understand why the Holy Spirit would request such a thing of me at a time when I was just really starting to get over it, and I also could not understand why He would want me to drag up the past and keep a record of it. Surely the Lord would want me to forget about such a period and move on with my life, I thought to myself.

I did not make a record on that particular day because I was still quite emotional about the whole thing. I was hurting at the time and I still had a few more issues that I needed to deal with. I can even remember telling the Holy Spirit that it was not necessary for me to write it down as I would never forget what I went through and I would always give the Lord thanks and praise for seeing me through.

The Holy Spirit, though, had other plans for my testimony and came back to me on the matter the following day with the same request, to record my testimony. Being obedient to His request, I eventually sat down and submitted myself to Him. "Lord," I prayed, "if this is really what you want me to do, please help me to write this because I cannot do it without You."

I sat in my living room for what seemed like days pouring out my heart onto the pages of my personal journal. The tears began to flow as the Holy Spirit brought things back to my memory, things that I had tried so desperately to erase. It was a very painful thing for me to do, but I continued despite the pain and tears.

After I had finished doing it I remember feeling so grateful that the Lord had saved me and I had an overwhelming feeling that I could do and overcome anything as long as He was with me.

At the time of first recording my testimony I had no idea what was to come next concerning these actions. After all, all I had done was write a list of bullet points about my experience into a personal journal — at least, that is all I thought I did!

For the next three or so years I kept this journal hidden underneath my sofa cushion in my living room, only looking at it two or three times after I had written it. Then one night in March 2007, the Holy Spirit led me to take it out with these words: "I am ready for you to use your testimony to minister to My broken-hearted women!" By now I knew better than to question the Lord's plans and instructions and I simply asked the Holy Spirit, "What do you want me to do with it?" And to this He replied, "I want you to write a book!"

Although I often hear my dad tell others about the great stories I used to write as a young child, I had never thought about writing a book before and if I were to listen to my mind I would have probably laughed my head off. I thank God for His word and I don't think it was a coincidence that one of the stories from the Bible that I had been meditating on for a couple of days prior to this moment was the one where the angel of the Lord visited Mary, the mother of Jesus. And He told her that she had been favoured by God and would be a virgin mother (*Luke 1:26-38*). The key parts of the text that had been at the forefront of my mind are verses 34 and 37, when Mary asked the angel "How could this be?" And then when she said "Never the less at your word let it be done." With these words still fresh in my mind it was easy for me to accept the Holy Spirit's surreal task for me (*see 2 Timothy 3:16-17*). And what can I say? The rest is history and here I am!

Recover it all! – 1 Samuel 30:8

My decision to write this book did not come about by accident — it was orchestrated by the Lord! And the things that I have shared with you so far are to give you a brief overview of my drama and the events that led up to the writing of this book. I also wanted you to understand where my compassion for broken-hearted women comes from.

As you read my story, my overall intention is to share with you all those real issues that I experienced, and I know that you will be truly blessed by my honesty and openness!

As my story unfolds on the following pages, I pray that you will enjoy it, learn from it, use it, believe it, and allow the Holy Spirit to speak to you through it. I have decided to give you the raw, undiluted version of what I went through, simply because I want you to be healed of your broken heart and free from your misfortune. My decision to give the uncensored version has not been an easy one to make, for a number of reasons, but the Lord as convinced me to do so and I totally trust His guidance.

As you read through my story I do not want you to feel sorry or sad for me in any way because I have overcome it; the Lord has totally healed me and I no longer suffer the deep pain of a broken heart. Instead, it is my desire that you will use my testimony as a turning point to trust in the Lord, who is in the business of changing the impossible (*Luke 1:37),* to heal your broken heart!

Send me Lord, I'll go! – 1 Samuel 17:32-58

Here is my story of what left me *absolutely broken-hearted* and completely overcome by grief and disappointment! It's the story that helped to push me into the arms of my Lord and Saviour, Jesus Christ *(Psalm 34:6),* the story that caused me to trust in the Lord for everything, and the story that turned my ashes into beauty *(Isaiah 61:3).* And for all of this I will always be eternally grateful and give all the glory to the Almighty Living God!

Chapter Two

But I thought it was Love!

In this chapter I am going to share some insight with you into the relationship that left me broken-hearted. Since this book is fundamentally about the Lord healing me of a broken heart and successfully moving me on from that period of my life, it is only right that I give you some history and insight into the relationship that left me so broken-hearted. In doing so I hope it will enable you to build a better understanding of where I am coming from, the depths of despair and pain that I experienced during this period of my life, and my personal first-hand experience, knowledge, and understanding of such an issue.

I do not know about you, but I usually find that it is a lot harder for me to listen to someone's advice or opinion on a subject if the person has not experienced it. I mean, how can you really understand something that you have never really experienced? Well, the fact is that I have personally experienced the raw, intense pain of a broken heart, and because of it I believe that I qualify to tell you, "Hold on in there, don't despair any longer, the Lord is on the scene and He will surely bring you through!"

As you read through my story you must remember that it is exactly that — my story. For this reason not everything I share with you may exactly reflect your situation, but I truly believe that the Lord has something for you in these pages or you simply would not be reading this book.

For those reading this book purely out of curiosity, those that have little understanding of how a man could leave you broken-hearted and those of you who believe that this could never happen to you, I have these words for you: "You may be surprised!" But for those of you who are desperately seeking a solution and answers to your problems, those that long to be whole again, those that personally know and understand the realisation of the effects of such an issue, keep reading, this is definitely a book that I believe will help and bless you.

It's History! – Psalm 126

Like most relationships mine did not start off as a bad relationship and no, I had no cause to believe that it would turn against me the way it did. From my personal experiences and observations it is fair to say that most relationships get off to a good start. Who in their right mind would go into a relationship if there were bad signs to start with? On second thought, forget that I made that comment, because nothing surprises me now!

In the beginning stages of a relationship the two parties involved are constantly trying to make the other party feel wanted, special, and loved. They will do things for each other that they would not normally do for anyone else. They will spend hours on the phone talking about everything and anything, and every free moment they have will be spent with each other. They will miss each other when they are not in each other's company, and they can do nothing wrong in each other's eyes because they are in a cloud called love. Must I go on? I am sure you get the picture.

In fact, before you read on, I want you to think about how you felt at such a time and add in the bits that I have left out, not because I did not experience them but because if I was to go down that road and fill in all the gaps, I would probably need to write a whole other book on the matter.

Well, the honeymoon beginnings of my relationship with this man were no different than what others experience on a daily basis. In other words, my situation was probably no different from yours!

From the day we first met there was something special between us. I know this because after we got together and started to share our feelings with one another, this is one of the things we spoke about. The initial linkup between us was a bit shaky for one reason or the other, but there was definitely a big attraction and a lot of chemistry between us. At this particular time I was quite young, about fifteen or sixteen, and I was not really looking for a boyfriend. But when I met and began to spend time with him my feelings began to warm towards the idea and they got stronger. Before I knew it I was in love with him.

I find it kind of funny now as I am looking back on that episode of my life because I can honestly say that I do not know exactly when I first fell in love with him — all I know is that I did. This was my first real relationship with a man, and it was also my first love. I had never been in love with a man before and I was not looking to fall in love with anyone either — it just happened!

A fair analysis of me at this time would read: "I was at a place where everything around me influenced me, and I did not take the time to question a lot of things that were happening in my life. I was just going with the flow of life and having lots of fun doing so."

So picture me, a young teenaged girl, not looking for a boyfriend but finding one anyway, and then falling head over heels in love with him. Does that sound like anyone you know?

Let us confront our pasts, coz the truth will set us free

Let me take you back to the beginning of my relationship, and I'll bet you can probably remember doing some of the things that I am about to share with you. We were inseparable. We just loved being in each other's company. Sometimes we did not do anything apart from sitting or lying down with one another, listening to music and joking around, but we were more than content doing so. *Isn't love just funny like that?* The more time I spent with him the more I began to trust him. And the more I began to trust him the more I began to share personal things with him — you know, the things you would not normally share with anyone. I must admit that I shared a lot more with him than he did with me, but that is simply because I am a woman and we need to talk and share things a lot more than men do. Don't worry about it, God made us this way.

The relationship became more and more intimate as time went on, and when I say intimate I am not just talking about the sexual side of it, I am talking about other areas too.

So I am in this relationship that I can only describe now as a rollercoaster relationship. Things were getting very intimate in the worldly sense, and everything seemed to be going well. But in reality, if I am honest, by this time the cracks were beginning to show. All was not as well as it seemed or as I would have liked to think.

It is funny because I say "reality," but how and with what do we really define reality with? What was reality for me back then is definitely not what I would call reality today!

Let me explain to you why I referred to this relationship as a rollercoaster relationship. And for those of you who have experienced a rollercoaster ride you will probably remember some of the following thoughts and feelings.

First there is the excitement and anxiety of plucking up the courage to first get on the ride. You can remember the other people getting off as you stood in line and the views and sounds of their reactions made you question your own capability to handle it. Then comes the feeling of sitting in the seat as the harness came over your head to lock you in. "Oh no, it's too late now," you tell yourself, "There's no turning back now." After all, you knew once you sat in the seat you had already committed yourself to it.

Next is the feeling that you were now in a position where you would have to experience all the things that this rollercoaster ride had to offer, whether they would be to your liking or not. Then come all the thoughts and feelings that bombarded your mind while you were experiencing the ride, some enjoyable and pleasant and some that were not so enjoyable and pleasant.

Last the feeling and thoughts of this ride coming to an end, anticipating how you would feel when it came to an end and how you would feel when you got off the ride. If you can remember, as you got off the ride, you too would have had a lot to say about it and would even advise others against or for it depending on how your experience went.

Well, my relationship with this man could most certainly be compared to a rollercoaster ride in the sense that sometimes we were in love, and sometimes we hated each other. Sometimes we would be on the phone for hours, sometimes we would not even call each other for days. Sometimes we were in lust, sometimes we couldn't stand to be near each other, sometimes we did everything together, and sometimes we wanted to be with our own friends. Sometimes we were very respectful and sometimes we were very disrespectful. Sometimes we were secure in each other; sometimes we were very insecure about each other. Sometimes we trusted each other and sometimes we did not trust each other — do you get the feeling of being on a rollercoaster yet?

Hindsight!

Several years on and looking back on my experience, I now recognize that this relationship was very addictive and unhealthy; it was simply bad for my health!

"Why have you come to this conclusion?" Someone may be asking. So let me explain.

In my opinion, which is now based on my knowledge and understanding of God's Word and the help and revelations given to me by His Holy Spirit, it was an addictive and unhealthy relationship simply because it was not the kind of relationship that the Lord had intended for me to be involved in. It did not glorify Him in any way at all. We glorify the Lord when we seek to know, obey, and carry out His known will in our lives, and this was not the case in this relationship.

It was during the time of this particular relationship that I began to seek the Lord by reading and meditating on His Words and learning His Ways. But I must admit, I was not very strong in the obeying part of this newfound relationship with Jesus Christ. In this, I mean that even after accepting Jesus Christ into my life and giving Him charge over it, the relationship with my then-boyfriend was still often rude, painful, knew no boundaries, did not follow Godly counsel, and to put it bluntly lacked commitment and vision.

When I say vision I mean that although I was in this relationship and claimed to love this man, I could not see myself ever committing to him in marriage for a number of reasons. The main reason was his lack of ability to carry out and follow through his words with accompanying actions. This part of the relationship really worried me, and I could not picture this man ever being my husband in his present state.

God's inspired Word show us in the book of Habakkuk, Chapter 2 verse 2 that we should have and write down our visions so that we can refer back to them for guidance in meeting our future goals. In other words, if we do not set goals in our hearts that we or the Lord have set for ourselves to achieve then we are running a race without any real reason to, so to speak.

Let us stop and think about this for a second: would you run a physical race if you knew the race did not contain a finish line? No, of course you would not, but in reality that's what many of us are actually doing in our lives.

One of the first things a runner will ask before beginning to run is, "How far will I have to run until I get to the finish line?" Our minds need to know these things from an early stage so we can prepare our bodies to deal with what we are about to put them through. God wants us to have this same mentality in running the race of life.

If you do not have a vision for the direction of your life, and this includes your relationships, you are basically living your life aimlessly without any firm goals in mind. And we know what the Word of God tells us about people living without Godly counsel or vision. It can be found in the book of Proverbs, Chapter 29 verse 18 and it reads as follows: *"where there is no vision, the people perish: but he that keepeth the law (God's law), happy is he"* (KJV).

God's will concerning how He prefers us to conduct our lives can be found in the Bible. This is His final Word and He will not change it to suit anybody — how can the creation dictate to its creator how it would like to be used? It is impossible, right?

At the time of starting this relationship I was not a Christian and therefore not familiar with the Bible or God's will for my life. Not having a relationship with the Lord meant that I was living life by my own standards and the standards of this world, and we all know that these standards are not stable and subject to change at any given time to suit our circumstances or public opinion.

I partially accepted Jesus Christ as my Lord and Saviour a few years into this relationship. The relationship, all in all, lasted for about six years, so I would say that for about three or four years out of the six I knew that I was compromising God's Word by disobeying His will and commandments. When I say that I partially accepted the Lord, what I mean is that even though I had made a commitment to give my life over to Jesus Christ to take charge of it, I was not totally committed to this decision and I continued to do a lot of things my own way, even when I knew it to be compromising in the eyes of God.

To be honest with you, I had consciously made up my mind to disregard God's ultimate unchangeable Word to fulfil my own needs, wants, and desires. And to put it even more plainly, my line of thinking was, "Lord, I love this man more than I will ever love You and nothing that You say will ever get me to live without him." (And can you believe that with this attitude, I even had the nerve to demand that the Lord honour my decision by helping me to keep my relationship with this man alive.)

Everyone is different and it is fair to say that there are not any two people in the whole world that have entirely the same DNA. We all have different experiences in life. Some have their share of good experiences and some bad. Some people are born with what seems like more chances than others and for some people it seems like they just don't stand a chance in this world. The ways in which people experience God's true nature and love are numerous as well. There are some people that are born into Christian families, there are some people who stumble into God's love, and then there are those that just seek to find and know Him.

Whatever the reasons, people usually find the Lord when they choose to. I am one of those people who found the Lord because I was desperate and needed some help, big time. Up until then I was not really looking for the Lord and did not feel like I needed Him — that is, until I was left broken-hearted and the pain got so overwhelming I thought I was going to die.

I thank the Lord that He is not like humans, in the sense that we hold grudges and count favours, or I would probably have died of my pain. I also delight in the fact and thank the Lord that you will not die in your pain either!

He is the only way! – John 14:6

A great woman of God first introduced me to the Lord in 1993. It was after one of those many times that I had yet another argument with my boyfriend. At the time I was feeling low, unhappy and hurt, and if I am honest I probably would have accepted anything that could have taken away my misery and depression and just cheered me up. So I listened to the offer of salvation that she was presenting to me. "If you have the Lord in your life Sasha," she used to say, "you will have a different kind of peace, a peace that is not determined by how someone else makes you feel!"

The source of the salvation in question is Jesus Christ *(see Romans 10:9)*. And when she used to speak these words to me, I can remember thinking to myself, this Jesus cannot help me in my situation because if I could not even help myself, how on earth could someone who had never even met me before be able to help me in my situation? My mind could not comprehend what she was saying, and the fact that I could not physically see this Jesus person did not help at all. Nevertheless, the words that she often spoke to me seemed so nice and comforting and I had nothing really to lose by reciting the salvation prayer with her, so I agreed to accept Jesus into my life.

This act was done partly because I had nothing to lose and partly to get her off my back, as she was always going on about me giving my life to the Lord Jesus Christ. I had spent a lot of time in her home with my boyfriend and thought that it would be polite of me to do as she wished. I am not really sure if at the time I really meant it, but like I said before, the Lord is only concerned with our hearts and He could tell if I really meant it or not. (God only knows if I meant it then, but somewhere along the line I must have meant it or else I would not be here writing about the love of God!)

My act of giving my life to the Lord and saying that salvation prayer must have happened on at least a hundred different occasions because at the time I did not understand that it was just something I had to do by faith and that I would not necessarily feel like something special had taken place. The Biblical definition of faith can be found in Hebrews 11:1 and simply means that we should have the confidence that what we hope for will actually happen when we believe and trust in the Word of God. It gives us the assurance that we have obtained the things we desire, even though we may not see them yet.

At this point, I believe that it is a good time to say that just because you do not feel saved when you call on the name of Jesus and believe that He died for you on the cross, does not mean that God has not accepted you as His own. It is a step of faith and you have to simply believe that something special has taken place in your life at that exact moment. Don't wait to feel like you are saved — you just are saved! Initially, I struggled with this concept because I did not read my Bible, and reading and hearing the Word of God is the key to believing and understanding this concept.

It takes some time to get your head around it, doesn't it? In your logical mind you ask questions such as, "Why would someone give you something for free and all you have to do is believe that they have given it to you?" And then on the other hand you say to yourself, "How can I believe in something I cannot see?"

Well I would like to tell you today that you no longer have to be confused about the mind and things of God. All you have to do is read your Bible regularly, talk to the Holy Spirit and ask Him to give you the wisdom and understanding you need to understand it!

From the year 1993 when I first gave my life to Christ up until 1997, the only time I wanted to know the Lord was when I needed His instant help and answer to a desperate matter, and this would mainly concern problems with my boyfriend. I cannot really remember any other thing that I prayed to the Lord about apart from this! Can you imagine how the Lord would have felt if He were a human being? He would have probably thought to Himself, "Why does this selfish little girl keep boring me with all her silly little prayers and requests?" or something along those lines. But seriously, the Lord obviously knew that if I continued to seek Him then one day He would be able to make Himself known to me, even if, to begin with, my seeking was for my own selfish reasons.

And sure enough, the Lord was right. When my world came crashing down towards the end of 1998, and I had nowhere else to turn, I ran to Him — my only option!

I honestly believe that it does not matter how a person comes to know the Lord. His ultimate desire is to have us all back in relationship and fellowship with Him. Nothing that you have done or experienced can make the Lord think any less of you. You are the apple of His eye *(Zachariah 2:8)* and He desires for you to walk in intimate relationship and fellowship with Him.

I am a living testimony that God loves those that did not love Him first, but I delight in the fact and thank the Lord that this is no longer the case for me.

There's a right way and there's a wrong way to do things!

Towards the end of 1998 my boyfriend and I had what was probably our millionth argument. I cannot remember what it was about or even who or what started it, but I do remember that I told him to get out of my life and leave me alone because I was fed up with the way things were going. In that argument a lot of hurtful things were said and we went our separate ways.

We were always arguing about something or another, but I noticed that after I had my son things seemed to get a lot worse. I am not really sure why this occurred but I think it is something to do with the fact that when you have a child of your own and are now responsible for someone else's well-being, you have to grow up fast and deal with it. The picture that I had painted in my mind before I had my son and the one that I was now experiencing were very different and it scared me, so I decided to do something about it.

Around this time I had been in college for about a year and was trying to make something of my life so that I could give my son a better standard of living and future. Social security benefits did not pay much and I had to try something fast because things were really starting to get me down. While pursuing my newfound career path I started to reflect on some areas of my life and what was really happening in them, and one of the areas that I looked into was my relationship. The more time that I spent thinking about it, the more I started to feel that I needed something more out of the relationship. But not once did I think that maybe I might be part of the reason things weren't going right. For me, the relationship just didn't seem that much fun anymore and it was beginning to feel like a noose around my neck. It just wasn't exciting anymore like in the 'good old days!'

This line of thinking eventually led to confusion, resentment, blaming, selfishness, and careless attitudes and behaviour on my behalf. I simply did not care anymore, at least not in the way I used to. A part of me did not really want to be in this relationship anymore and another part knew no better and was prepared to stay in it for the sake of social appearance. One of my lines of thinking was that I might not be totally happy with him, but that I was quite sure in the fact that I did not want anyone else to have him. I mean, he was all I knew as a boyfriend and we had grown up together. How would I cope seeing him with someone else?

This mindset had mainly developed because over the past years in the build-up to this moment I had often challenged the interest of other girls who tried to tempt him away, and was I really prepared to give him up now! He was gorgeous, had a very caring nature, and made me feel like no one else had ever made me feel. However, where these particular factors had been a strong line of reasoning to me previously, they did not seem to be so strong to me at this point. I had arrived at the stage in the relationship where I began thinking to myself, "Do I really want to be with this person anymore and do I even love him anymore?" This was a very confusing time for me because previously I had always believed for sure that I would never want to leave this man no matter what, and now I was contemplating initiating the split.

By now I had found myself at a very strange place both mentally and physically and because of this I was unable to make a final decision that I felt I could stick to and live with. I was totally confused at this point!

In the years that we had been together he had appeared to have such genuine qualities and characteristics and I had grown to love him for them, but when I needed him to demonstrate these things he just could not seem to deliver. For years I had felt safe with this man and I had believed that I could trust him with my very life, but by this point I was no longer feeling safe and secure with him. I was even starting to question whether or not he had me or our son's best interests at heart. I had pondered these thoughts and feelings for some time in the lead-up to this moment, but would always suppress them. But in the heat of the moment, during an intense argument, they came out in my rage and anger.

The particular day in question does not stand out to me anymore, and

I cannot remember that much about the actual events of that day or night. Even as I sit here trying to share these details with you they just don't stand out to me anymore. All I can remember is that it was some time before my birthday in November when we had this argument and that I was very cold towards him. I told him that I did not want to be with him anymore so he should just leave me alone. The reason I remember that it was sometime in October was because in the following month, November, I had a birthday party to celebrate my twenty-fourth birthday and almost everyone that attended kept asking me where he was or what time he was coming. I remembered feeling so hurt that he hadn't even phoned me to wish me happy birthday or anything. In all the years that I had known him he had never missed my birthday.

On the day or night that we had the argument, I can remember thinking to myself that if I got all my hidden feelings out in the open it would somehow give me the courage to do the thing that I had thought about doing for months. I had dreamed of ending the relationship for so long and this somehow seemed like the excuse that I needed to do it. (It is kind of funny how we often find it much easier to do something that we would not normally be able to do when we are acting in anger.)

Looking back on this occasion, I wish that I had done things a lot differently. I wish I had not treated him the way that I did, but for some silly reason I thought that the only way to end a relationship was negatively. After all, why would you end a relationship with someone if you still wanted to be friends with them? I know differently now, but at the time I was too immature to fully comprehend this possibility.

Anyway, the bottom line was that we were not getting on and by now we were not agreeing on anything. He would say A and I would say B; he liked this and I liked that. The only thing that we did seem to agree on by this time was sex, but even that was becoming negative, so what else could I have done in such circumstances?

So was this what I really wanted?

The first few weeks were fine, and as the weeks progressed into months we had very little contact with one another and the contact we did have was usually minimal and straight to the point. I had my young son and college assignments to keep me busy and this helped to keep my mind from dwelling on my current break-up for too long. I would be lying to you, though, if I said it did not hurt a bit at this stage. If I am honest, it was like I had just separated from my best friend and a big part of my heart had been cut away. This person had been in my life for as long as I could remember and we had been really close.

Initially the break up did not seem to hurt me too much and my heart had not been broken at this stage. I think I had felt this way because I was still quite angry with him and I felt that this was all for the best. At various points in my relationship I had experienced feelings of being trapped, manipulated, and controlled by my partner, and for the first time in ages I was starting to experience the feeling of freedom again.

When you are in a relationship with someone else you have to take his or her views, feelings, and opinions into account in order for the relationship to run as smoothly as possible. In the beginning I totally valued his views, feelings, and opinions because he seemed much more experienced than I was. But as I grew up and started to experience things for myself I began to feel that his views, feelings, and opinions were governing the way I felt about myself, the way I carried myself, and the choices that I made.

Initially, after the split first took place this was one of the areas I longed to explore — my freedom! I started to make a point of doing things that I had wanted to do but would often get questioned by him for doing, such as wanting to go away for the weekend without having my motives for doing so examined. I took advantage of my newfound single status and not having to answer to anyone for my actions, and I seemed to be enjoying it. However, although I was enjoying this time, I was also finding it a bit strange. I had been in a relationship with this person since my mid-teens, and I was finding it a bit weird being on my own and having to fend for a small son and myself.

Although my situation had changed and I was now single, my mindset was struggling to catch up with my actual status. In reality I was single, but in my mind I was still attached to this person by some strong unseen connection. *Anyway, this is not a problem,* I thought to myself. *I don't want to go too far and upset him to the point where we could not possibly get back together* was my line of reasoning. Like I mentioned before we were always breaking up and getting back together and I did not really perceive that this time would be any different than the rest. I thought *If I really don't like being on my own, I will just give him a call and we'll talk and realise how much we love and miss each other,* and eventually we would get back together again. This had been a familiar cycle and pattern that I had grown used to for the past five or six years, and it had worked many times before, so why would this time be any different?

My whole world came crashing down!

I do not recall exactly when the wind was sucked out from beneath my wings and my whole world came crashing down, but it happened a few months after we initially split up, so it must have been sometime in early 1999.

The man that I had known and gave my whole being to, including my heart, the man that I had so desperately loved more that anything in the whole wide world, had started a new relationship. And one of the most hurtful things for me to deal with at this time was the fact that he did not tell me himself. Instead I heard it from someone else who had assumed that I would have known by now.

I was in total shock! My whole being from that moment on became numb and my heart felt like someone had just stabbed me straight through the middle of it. And what I did not know at this moment was that these feelings were going to stay with me like an unwanted visitor for the next few years. I struggled to comprehend how someone you have totally trusted with all your heart and being could do this to someone he claimed to have loved with all his heart. And it was at this point that my heart slowly began to break!

It was a feeling and experience that really knocked the life out of me; a feeling and experience that will always be one of the most memorable moments of my life. The pain that I experienced was very deep and uncomfortable. And unless you have ever experienced such pain first-hand you could never possibly understand it!

A million things began to go through my mind at this point. It was as though I was standing outside my body and looking in at a person that I did not even recognise. And I could not seem to grasp that this was actually happening to me.

How did it come to this? I kept asking myself. *Lord, why did you not warn me? What am I going to do now? Is he just trying to get back at me for that night we argued? Why did I treat him that way? Why could I not be satisfied with what I had? Why did I want more?*

My list of questions and reasons were endless and nothing or no one could make me feel any worse than I did at this point. From that moment on this issue became the centre of my universe and everything else came after, including the Lord, my son, my college course, and me.

The fact that he did not personally tell me about his new relationship somehow gave me a false sense of hope. My mind would tell me that the reason why he had not told me yet was because it was not actually true. So I chose to believe this line of thinking because it was the one that made me feel a little better. But the suspense was getting to me, so after a short while after first hearing the news about this new relationship I finally plucked up the courage to ask him directly if it was true. It was one of those occasions when you want to ask a question but you're not really sure if you are ready to hear the answer. Not knowing the truth was hurting me badly enough, so I thought to myself, *Can knowing the truth possibly hurt anymore than this does?*

Before asking him the question I had not believed that it could possibly hurt much more, but after I asked him and he confirmed it to me I felt a million times worse than I thought I would. By now my heart was not just severely wounded, it was slowly dying! And I will never forget the way I felt physically and emotionally — I felt awful.

Even after the truth had been revealed to me and everything was out in the open, for some reason I still entered into a state of unbelief and denial. And this state would come and go at intervals for years to come afterwards. The pain that I was experiencing was so overwhelming that it seemed to make me feel better if I simply followed the line of believing that this had not actually happened to me.

It sounds silly to say this now, but that is actually what I chose to do at times to cope with my pain in the situation. I use the term "at times" because there were occasions when I would speak to my ex-partner and he would spell it out to me loud and clear, that he was now with someone else. And when he was not telling me so, my own mind would highlight these facts at every possible opportunity. So it really did not matter how far I would go in my attempts to try and block it all out, there was always something or someone there to remind me that this was actually a reality. And worse still, it was happening to me!

The feeling of rejection followed my initial emotions of unbelief and denial. I had experienced this feeling long before as a young child at primary school with my friends. It was one I had known well and could identify with: the feeling of being turned away by the one you most wanted to be with. This time it was a million times worse than the rejection I had experienced as a young child in the school playground. This time my entire heart was involved! As young as I was in that playground, I somehow seemed to cope with their rejection, but as an adult, I did not seem to be coping too well with this dose of rejection. Another issue that contributed to my pain was the fact that everyone else seemed to know what was going on, and in some cases they even knew more than I did about what was going on. I struggled to cope with the fact that others knew more than I did. And of course, I made this a hundred times worse with my own speculations and lines of thought, and this in turn led to me losing some of the trust I had in some people. To sum it up in a few words, my worst nightmare had just begun and I had the lead part in it — and not by choice, may I add!

This issue that I now know to be so minor was magnified by both myself and the devil into something that overtook every waking moment of my life. And I really do believe that it was a strategic attempt of the devil to stop me from reaching my divine destination!

You may not know it yet, but the Lord really does care for you

After the breakdown of this relationship, one of the options that I had was to learn from my painful mistakes, so I decided to find out what the Word of God had to say about relationships and why mine had hurt me so badly. I chose to do this because I thought that by having these answers it would help to make me feel better and help with my recovery. What I mean is that if I could at least find some answers to where I went wrong, I would be less likely to make the same painful mistakes again. The bottom line was that I needed some answers to explain my pain so that I could begin to understand and get over it! One of the other reasons I chose to do this was because I was determined that I was not going to let myself get hurt like that again, not if I could help it! (When you go through something that nearly knocks the life out of you it makes you very cautious of allowing the same thing to occur again.)

In my seeking to find some answers for my pain I began to do the things that I should have been doing before as a believer of Christ. I read my Bible regularly, listened to tapes, read and listened to other people's similar testimonies, observed and studied the relationships of others and talked to the Holy Spirit about this subject. Over a period of time my knowledge and understanding of the Lord and this issue began to grow and increase.

I do not remember the exact day when the Holy Spirit led me to 1 Corinthians Chapter 13, but He used it to explain to me what having "love" for someone else really entails. As you take time to read through and study this passage of Scripture and you really meditate on and think about what these words mean, it is not hard to see that our definition of "love" and God's definition of "love" are totally different.

In a nutshell, human love is conditional and based on what the other person can do for you, and it is this factor that will determine what you are prepared to do for them. Whereas God's love, the ultimate definition of love, is unconditional and based on the fact that, regardless of what you do for me, I am going to keep finding a way to love you to the end no matter what. It is an eternal commitment! At first I could not understand this concept and found it hard to comprehend how this could be possible, but the more time I spent in the Word of God and getting to know His Way and how He thinks and operates, I am now able to understand and appreciate God's definition of "love."

By simply meditating on those verses and allowing the Holy Spirit to teach me step by step, I soon realised that what I thought I was presenting to this other person wrapped up in a package with a tag called "love" was not really love at all. OK, it was a worldly kind of love, but it was not a Godly kind of love. God's love is not supposed to hurt or be painful and this relationship and love did hurt and it was painful!

You choose!

"So if the Lord really cares about us, why does He allow such things to happen to us?" Someone may be asking right now.

My answer to this question is simple and based on my personal experiences, knowledge, and understanding, to date, of God's Character and Word. God does not want to see the women He has created go through such painful experiences. It grieves Him to see us broken-hearted and in pain!

The Lord wants to have a personal relationship with each of us so He can show and teach us a way that will prevent us from experiencing these unnecessary things. Unfortunately, like me, most of us fail to see the need for the Lord until we are down and out, in pain, or desperate, and even then, we often still find it hard to simply trust Him, or take Him at His Word and follow His Way.

I came to this conclusion as a result of my growing relationship with the Lord and through reading my Bible. God will not go against or override our own will, He simply cannot do it!

In the book of Deuteronomy (30:19) the Word of God presents us a choice: *life or death.* The choice that we make is ultimately up to us, not God. Let me illustrate to you how much the Lord really loves and wants to help us with our lives.

Although the Lord has left this choice up to us, in the same verse He goes on to suggest what He would wish for us all to choose. It says, *"Oh, that you would choose life, so that you and your descendants might live!"* (NLT) God created us with our own free will and He will not take this gift back!

In this verse we can clearly see that unless we choose to live life God's Way, we are inevitably choosing death. Therefore, we should not really complain when we see death manifesting in certain areas of our lives, such as in a broken relationship like mine. It is a painful lesson to learn, but it is the truth! God cannot help us if we will not read His word, listen to His voice and obey His Ways, and that's the bottom line!

Imagine if God changed His Word and mind every time He wanted to suit Himself or our circumstances. Apart from the fact that He would not be any better than a human being, we as humans would not have any respect for Him.

The Lord can only get involved in our lives if we personally invite Him to do so, and at the time I experienced my heartache I had not given Him an invitation.

For God so loved the world that He gave His only begotten Son . . . (John 3:16-21)

Before I end this chapter, the Holy Spirit has instructed me to present you with an opportunity for you to accept His gift of salvation. In other words, He wants to begin a personal relationship with you.

I encourage you right now, if you have not already asked Jesus Christ into your heart or you simply wish to renew your heart and life back to Him, to say this simple prayer out loud with me. It is a simple prayer that will open the door for the Lord Jesus Christ to enter into your life and help you to live a life that is pleasing to God (*please read Romans 10:8-13*).

Jesus Christ, I thank you for dying on the cross for me and my sins and I surrender my life, heart and will to you today. I ask that you will come into my life from this moment forth and allow Your Holy Spirit to guide and lead me through this life – In the name of Jesus, I thank you God for this transition into Your Kingdom. **Amen**

Chapter Three

myspace.com/sashataylor
The Pain!

On the night I first recorded this testimony in November 2003, the Holy Spirit spoke these words to me: "Sasha, your testimony will never be really effective and help to set others free if you don't share the fullness of it with them."

At the time I did not fully comprehend what the Holy Spirit meant in making such a statement or why He would even make these words known to me, but all the same I proceeded to record them alongside my testimony. I had known for about two years prior to this announcement that one day He would want me to share my story in order to help others with their situations, but in my mind I presumed that the simple bits that I would choose to share would be on my terms.

At this point I did not have any intention of sharing it all with anyone. The truth is that I was too wrapped up in myself to care about what someone else was going through, and my first and only priority was to find deliverance and healing for myself!

Back then I could not even begin to imagine how the Lord could possibly heal my broken heart, much less think about how He would use my story to help others. I was so concerned with the Lord's ability to deliver and heal my own heart that the thought of speaking out and sharing the fullness of my story with others never crossed my mind. You can call me naïve, but I honestly believed that the Lord would somehow find a way to use my simple account of events to help others out of their situations. And I would say to myself things like, *surely the Lord knows me better than anyone and can read my mind, and He knows full well that I would never ever consider sharing the fullness of my experience with anyone.* I thought it would be our secret forever!

For further clarification on this matter, let me just put it this way: if the Lord had told me back in 2003 that the reason He was asking me to keep a written record of my experience was so that one day I could use it as the blueprint for a book about my heartbreak I would never have agreed to record it. And the fact that the Lord knew this was probably why He only revealed part of the plan to me and not His entire intentions *(see Isaiah 55:8-9)*.

Mindsets!

From 2003 up until around March 2007, my mindset was that one day I would do what the Lord had asked me to do and share my story with others, but it would be done in the simplest way possible without too much detail. And according to me, not even the Lord could persuade me to do it any differently. Nevertheless, I did not let this line of thinking stand in the way of my relationship with the Lord and I still continued to seek and stay close to Him.

I find that the Lord is good like that. He never pressures us into doing anything that we do not want to do, despite the fact that He could do so if He really wanted to. He simply leaves the choices and decisions up to us, but for some silly reason we seem to forget that He is an all-knowing God and He knows what we will do long before we ever think or choose to do it.

What I am trying to say is that when I had made up my mind not to tell the fullness of my story, the Lord already knew that the day would come when I would actually feel differently about the matter, so there was no need for Him to pressure me or convince me otherwise. The Lord knew that a day would come when I would be at a place in my relationship with Him, where I would trust Him enough to do anything that I could to give Him all the glory, help others and further His Kingdom.

Helpful advice?

When you are going through something that is very personal to you, like dealing with the pain of a broken heart, there will definitely be others, usually in your own circle of friends, there to advise you and say things like, "Stop being so silly! How could you get yourself in such a state over a man? You're pretty enough — get another man! Get over it and stop acting stupid," and so forth. In such cases you have to remember that these individuals are your friends and they generally want to see you out of your depression or sadness. And although it may not be what you want to hear at the time because of the inner pain that you are experiencing, you must understand that they are just trying to help you in the best way they know how.

I experienced such advice during my distress and this triggered a battle in my mind. My battle was between choosing to believe what the Holy Spirit was saying to me and what my family and friends were saying to me. At the height of my trial and pain there was a period where I was torn between trusting the people that I had known all my life and trusting the Lord that I was just beginning to become acquainted with. Also I must add that my newfound relationship and dependency on the Lord during this time had merely arisen out of my desperation in an extreme time of need and not from any real desire in me to truly know Him.

I spent many years of my life ruled by both the voice of the Holy Spirit and the voice of others and it was like being on a playground see-saw. One minute I would be more on the side of the Holy Spirit and the next I would be more on the side of my family and friends' views and opinions. Sometimes I would listen to my friends' advice on my matter and sometimes the Holy Spirit's, and in all my listening I was completely perplexed and in a constant state of confusion.

As a believer in the Lord I did not believe or understand that if my friends' opinions or advice did not line up with the Word of God or with what the Holy Spirit was saying to me, that my best bet would be to just disregard it. Instead I spent a lot of unnecessary time considering many things that I simply did not need to consider. For example, my friends and family would tell me that the fact that my ex-boyfriend had moved on to a new relationship meant that it was the right and acceptable time for me to do so, but when I would ask the Holy Spirit if this was alright with Him, He would say, "No," "Wait," "You are not ready yet," so then all confusion would begin in my mind because I would start to question the Holy Spirit's reasons for saying "No" and "Wait" and compare them to what was acceptable to the world.

Nevertheless, I did not choose to go against the Lord on this matter for the obvious reason that I had been left so badly hurt by my previous relationship and I was not about to go down the same road again. If I am honest with you, there were many occasions when I did feel like starting a new relationship and I could easily have done so, but I chose not to because deep down I knew that the Holy Spirit was right in what He was saying and I wasn't ready.

I desired to be free!

Most people's lives are dominated by how others view them. They want to portray a persona that others will like, and I was very much like that. On the surface I was very good at presenting and portraying the picture of someone that had it all together. At least, this is how I believe that I came across to others most of the time! I was good at this and I worked really hard at concealing the real extent of my pain from others because I was so embarrassed by the way that I was handling my situation.

The bottom line is that no one really wants to be around someone that is always negative or depressed and down in the dumps, not unless he or she is in the same place and needs someone else to join in the pity party.

There was a time when I used to feel that having the company of others was paramount and it was for this reason that I had subconsciously decided to portray a got-it-all-together act to the outside world. I was afraid that if I had let certain people see my true condition at this time then they would not have wanted to be around me. They would have talked about me, they would have laughed at me and they would not have understood my pain.

Trust in the Lord with all your heart . . . Proverbs 3:5-6

One of the first Scriptures I ever memorised was Proverbs 3:5-6 and I love this Scripture even now. I used to meditate on it all the time and relate it to almost every situation that I was going through in my life during that period. I was so excited that I knew and could quote this Scripture because there were times when the Holy Spirit would bring it back to my memory just in the nick of time, and I would be encouraged at the thought of it. These times were usually when I felt like I could not stand anymore or when I believed that I was going to totally crumble under all the pressure. These Scripture verses were so comforting to me: *"Trust in the Lord with all your heart; do not depend on your own understanding. Seek his will in all you do, and he will show you which path to take"* (NLT).

For me Proverbs 3:5 and 6 meant that I would somehow need to learn to completely trust the Lord in the best way that I possibly could and not rely on my own understanding of my present situation. And I would have to do this if I really wanted my life to be whole again.

Trusting someone else can be a hard thing to do, especially if, like me, you have been left badly shaken and hurt as the result of trusting a loved one not to let you down. I could not help it and I found this concept very difficult to do at the beginning of my relationship with the Lord. I struggled with simply trusting in Him because I could not believe and take the Lord at His Word. I was comparing the Almighty God to the man that had hurt me, and how wrong I was!

It was only when I started to believe in and follow these instructions by means of submitting my heart to the Lord that He could then prove to me that I could trust Him in all things. But again, like most worthwhile things, this took time.

As rightly stated in Proverbs Chapter 3, it was only as I continued to seek the Lord that I was able to get to know and understand Him and believe in His Word. Not only did seeking to develop my relationship with the Lord enable me to do this but it also helped me to really see Him for what He truly is: totally trustworthy and faithful to His Word!

"What do you mean when you use the term that you continued to seek Him?" Someone may be asking right now. So let me explain this a little further for you.

I would talk to the Lord just as if I was talking to someone physically seated right there next to me. I was totally honest with the Lord and told Him what I was feeling and why. (You may as well tell Him as He knows all things anyway!) I attended church regularly which was great for my growth and development at the time because I was a "Sunday Bible reader" and I only really opened my Bible on a Sunday during the service.

The fact that I regularly attended church was very useful for me at that stage of my relationship with the Lord as I was able to hear the Word of God concerning various life issues, keep notes, and occasionally refer back to some of the Scriptures that I had heard when I needed to revisit them again. I kept in close contact with a mature Christian friend who had proven herself trustworthy to me. I knew that she would be able to encourage and pray for me when I really needed it. And I also watched Christian videos and television because I liked hearing the stories and testimonies of how and where the Lord had delivered other people from.

However, my biggest past-time with the Lord was, still is, and forever will be listening to music. I am a person who, as far back as I can remember, loves to listen to music. The feeling and pleasure that I get from listening to music can only be likened to that of going on a peaceful personal journey into another realm!

Listening to the voices of many of the Lord's anointed music ministers singing and ministering His sweet Words and heart to me without a doubt helped me to experience my deliverance, comfort, and God's love and healing power. I honestly do not know where I would be today if it were not for my genuine love of music!

Who the Son sets free is free indeed! – John 8:36

"Why would you make up your mind not to share the fullness of your testimony with others, if you knew that the Lord would one day expect this of you?" Someone may be asking

I began to answer this question for you earlier on in this chapter and would like to finish it off by adding that during this particular moment in my life I was still at a place where what others thought or said about me determined and dictated the outcome of my actions. Back then in the early stages of my experience I cared more about what others would have to say about my story than I did about giving the Lord all the glory for what He had done for me!

It has taken me a good while, but I have now come to a place where I no longer solely care about what others may think about me, whether they would have done things differently or not, whether or not they believe or like me or not, what their opinions might be concerning these things that I have written, whether they will laugh at my distress or not, whether I will feel embarrassed to share my story, whether I may be ashamed or even what the world may have to say concerning my sincerity. I simply choose to be obedient to the Lord and the leading of the Holy Spirit because I have all cause to believe and deem Him as trustworthy and for these reasons Lord please use me – *my life is no longer my own; use me for Your glory!*

Oh my Lord . . . you really do want me to share everything!

When the Holy Spirit first asked me to record my story I did so as bullet points. I sat down with my pen in hand and asked the Holy Spirit to help me remember some of the raw details. Like I stated before, at the point of first recording my testimony I did not know the Holy Spirit's reasons for asking me to do this. Never in my wildest dreams did I ever think the record I made would one day be the framework for a book based on my personal experiences. So as I sit here writing this book, I cannot help but delight in the fact that because of my obedience at that time, the Lord is now using me to be a blessing to others.

The Holy Spirit has suggested to me that I should include some of the actual bullet points He helped me record. At first I was a bit reluctant to do it and I had to really mull over it but I have thought about it quite a bit and have decided that I would actually like you to see some of these bullet points as they were first written. My choice to share these bullet points with you in this way will give me the opportunity to be as open with you as I possibly can.

The Lord's purpose for me to write this book is so that He can show others that He is able to heal a broken heart. For this reason alone I may as well keep it real with you and give Him all the glory. The words that you are about to read are sincerely from my heart, and the fact that they were initially written for my eyes only means that they have not been toned down in any way. I really believe that you will benefit from them and begin to appreciate my overall intentions for writing this book.

These bullet points are presented exactly as I first wrote them and may not be coherent on their own. As most of the statements are quite brief and straight to the point, I have decided to give further explanations and in some cases reflections directly below each point. My overall desire is to do what I know the Lord will expect of me by going forth and sharing the fullness of my story with you.

In the process of writing this book I have struggled with my fleshly desire to water down my story by not making it sound too embarrassing, but the Holy Spirit has helped me to deal with this. And although it has been an agonising struggle for me, I have decided that I want to follow the lead of the Holy Spirit and give the Lord all the glory!

I have titled this chapter "myspace.com/sashataylor - The Pain!" because everything you will read in the rest of this chapter is to permit you full access into "my space and my pain!" I will allow you to take a look behind the scenes at the extent of the pain and distress that I experienced during that period of my life and I hope that my openness and honesty will truly bless you!

"Holy Spirit please give me the strength to share this with others, help me to make you proud of me and to let your name be glorified in all of this." (This will be my constant prayer of encouragement for myself as I continue to write the rest of this book.)

The Pain!

Before I go on to share with you some of the painful things that I personally experienced, let me quickly attempt to recreate the picture of the place where I was the night I first recorded theses bullet points.

At the time, my ex-boyfriend and I had been finished for about four years. I was at a point where I was just starting to get over my broken heart and I was making good progress. I was starting to depend more and more on the Lord and He was helping me to get my life together. I was getting physically and emotionally stronger, but I still had some way to go. My depression was starting to lift and I had finally conquered my unhealthy desire to have sex with my ex-partner. I was feeling much better than I had in ages! I still had some way to go, but the fact that I could now see a light at the end of the tunnel was a great turn-around for me.

While talking to the Holy Spirit one evening, He asked me to write in my journal what I had been through. I was mystified why He would ask this of me and told Him that it was not necessary. "Let's just forget it," I remember saying to the Holy Spirit that night. The Holy Spirit came back to me the following evening, for the second time, with the same request to record my story in my journal.

I did not do it the first time He asked because I was a bit surprised that He would want me to do such a thing but when He asked me to do so a second time, I decided that I would be obedient *(see 1 Samuel 15:22)*. The thought of actually doing it was quite daunting and I had a sick feeling in my stomach that everything which I had tried so hard to suppress and bury was going to be brought right back to the surface to pull me back under again.

OK Holy Spirit, I thought to myself, *let's get on with it*. And with my journal and pen in my hand I sat and waited on the Holy Spirit to guide me through the process because I really did not want to or know how to do it.

This is such a painful experience, I thought to myself, *but what have I got to lose — I mean apart from my mind?* And with this in my mind the words and tears began to flow as the Holy Spirit started taking me back through painful memories and I wrote these words . . .

- *Fear, shame, vivid memory, embarrassment are a few of the reason why I have not been able to share my testimony that actually changed my focus from me to God.*

At this time there were a number of things that prevented me from even dreaming about sharing my experience with others. The first factor was the fear of allowing anyone to know how vulnerable, defenceless, and weak I felt during this time. This feeling was so overwhelming that it governed all my other feelings, and it even governed my life itself. This was hard for me to deal with because I am normally a lively, outspoken, and up-front type of person and if I am honest I quite like these qualities about myself. I guess it would be even fairer to say that I pride myself on these characteristics! However, the downside of this, during the time of my distress, was that others still expected me to be like this.

Fear was one of the major influences in my mind during this period. There was the fear of change, the fear of moving on, the fear of what other people would say, the fear of not knowing any different, the fear of making another wrong move, the fear of not being able to cope, the fear of having to raise my son on my own, the fear of someone else getting what was meant for me, the fear of being out of God's will, the fear of seeing my ex-boyfriend happy with someone else, and there was even the fear of him having another baby with his new girlfriend. To be honest, the fears were actually endless and would increase on a daily basis until my head felt like it was going to literally explode with the pressure of so much fear.

Another reason for me believing that I could not possibly share my story with anyone was the great sense of embarrassment that I had felt. The fact that I had seen others go through break-ups and seemingly cope with it a lot better than me made me feel inadequate. (I mean, what advice could I possibly give someone else concerning their situation if I could not even get over my own heartbreak?) I was embarrassed about the way I took things, about the way I reacted to situations and conducted myself, and about the way I continued to compromise the Lord's will for my life.

It is fair to say that there are some things that we don't mind sharing with others and that most of the time these are usually the things that will not cause us too much embarrassment. For years I believed that sharing my story would only cause me a lot of embarrassment and I did not see any point in doing so. However, as time has gone on and I have grown up in the Lord my focus has shifted from myself to the Lord. I have grown to understand that there is a need for me to bypass superficial things such as fear and embarrassment and look forward to the bigger picture: the need to give help and a sense of hope to other broken and hurting people!

Today, all grown and mature in the things of God, I now realise that everything we personally go through can be used to help someone else in some way or another. For example, because I am open and honest with you and sharing my story, I believe others will receive hope, healing, and a purpose for living as a result of hearing my testimony. It is for this reason that I choose to help you, and the more I press on and write these words the more the feelings of embarrassment and fear fade into the background. But the truth is, though, that it did cause me a lot of pain initially and I do fully understand why and how people end up struggling with this area!

- *Nobody (not even those on my side) could help me to overcome the pain and hurt that I was feeling.*

Have you ever been in a crowded room full of close friends and family but you still feel like you are the only one in the room? It seems like an impossible scenario, but this is exactly how I felt. Obviously there were people around me that could see some of the pain that I was going through, but no one could have possibly comprehended the full extent of the pain and hurt that I was experiencing.

Such a place is so personal to any individual and no one can possibly help you get through every negative emotion and the levels of pain you are experiencing. They probably would if they could but the truth is that no human being has the capacity to fully understand what another is going through.

This was one of the loneliest times of my life. I was not lonely because I was literally on my own. Instead, it was more like an inner sense of feeling alone with nowhere to go and no one to turn to for an instant fix.

The fact that I could not turn to anyone, even though there were plenty of people around me, really forced me to draw closer to the Lord. I had never felt this way before and at the time I found it very hard to deal with.

In a way my pain became my blessing in disguise, as it proved to me that there is only one person that is really able to give me everything that I need to function — the Lord. And who knows, maybe if I was not on my face and in so much pain, my relationship with Him wouldn't be what it is today. (I probably will never really know the true answer to this line of thought, but I am pretty sure that things would be different for me right now.)

- *I cried ... and cried ... and cried ... and to make matters worse I went off my food, in fact could not eat properly if I wanted to because I could not stomach food.*

There was a period in the earlier stages where all that I could do was cry and this period seemed to go on forever. It did not matter how hard I tried to look on the bright side, a time would always eventually come where I would emotionally crumble under the pressure of everything. This usually occurred on a daily basis. I cannot remember how many days and nights I spent crying my heart out to the Lord, but the tears sown could have filled an ocean.

I was and still can be a very emotional person but at the time this was the only way I knew how to express my pain. During that era of my life I was very emotional and I used to let my emotions govern my life. I could not cope with the overwhelming feeling of grief and helplessness. I even remember the times when I would cry at the slightest thoughts that came into my mind, and I would be left drained by them.

The other issue I could not control was the fact that I went off food whenever I was stressed. This was not by choice as I do love food, but it was something that just happened to me. There were times when I felt so hungry and would have loved to eat but something in my mind would tell me, *you cannot eat that!* Or, *if you eat that you are going to be sick.* I would get to a stage where I could not stomach the thought of actually eating food, so I would eat small snacks just to help me make it through the days. There were some days that I would eat a little and some days when I would not eat anything at all. This pattern lasted for what seemed like a lifetime and could have possibly been a few years but, like I said before, God carried me through.

Pain can attack individuals in many ways and I guess this was just one of the ways it attacked me. Other people experiencing pain say that they eat for comfort and therefore put on a lot of weight, I guess it just depends on the individual.

- *This led to me losing a lot of weight (I must mention that I have never been a large girl at any time in my life so you can imagine how I looked). This outward manifestation brought comments from others on the state of my weight, which in turn made me feel so ugly and it did not help me in any way.*

Now you do not have to be a genius to know that if you don't eat you are more than likely to lose weight and your body will not get the nutrients it needs to stay healthy.

My body framework is quite slim and I am about five feet nine inches tall, and up until my weight plunged, I had never been any other way. The fact that I could not eat much meant that I began to lose weight rapidly. My clothes size dropped from a size twelve to a size eight and to put it quite bluntly I looked like a skeleton in clothes. I hated the way I looked because I knew this was not me but at the same time I also felt powerless to do anything about it.

The things on the inside of you can be disguised or covered up but unfortunately the same cannot be said for outer appearance. Everyone gets to see that. It is on show for others to see and comment on and that is exactly what they did in my case. My family and friends would comment on the state of my weight and the fact that I was not looking too well.

I know that they were just sharing a fact with me and I also knew that their motives were not bad, but really this did not help me in any way. I knew that the state of my weight was not good, but the fact that others were commenting on it made me feel ten times worse than I did to begin with, and before I knew it I began seeing myself as ugly.

- *The devil would let up (usually when I was doing other pointless things with others) but as soon as I was by myself he was there to taunt me over and over and over again.*

This bullet point refers to the fact that during this time the devil really tried his utmost best to bury me alive.

In John10:10 the Bible tells us that the job of the devil is to destroy God's children before they can achieve what He wants them to personally achieve in this world. And of course, I was not exempt from this persecution.

For months and months and years and years the devil oppressed me to the point of destruction. He would suggest things to my mind that would make me a nervous wreck and give me images that I did not wish to see. The taunting was endless and it would start right from the point of me waking up until the point of sleep that next night.

This was a draining period both physically and emotionally, but by the grace of God I was able to get from one day to the next. There were some days that I would be so physically and emotionally exhausted that I could not even pick myself out of bed, but I would reluctantly do so for the sake of my son and my studies.

- *At this point I was sinking fast (I even contemplated suicide). "God help me please" – I would cry out almost constantly.*

When you are constantly feeling down and depressed and cannot seem to see a way out of your mess, a part of you may come to the point where you say, "What is the point continuing with life?" or, "What have I got to live for?" Well, there were times when I came to this junction. I got so low that I got to the point where I started to contemplate suicide as a way out of my pain.

I used to sit and think about how peaceful it would be if I took my life and went to be with the Lord, and what it would feel like if I did not have to deal with all this turmoil anymore. I used to sit and dream about being somewhere far away where there was no more pain and it really sounded good to me. I would sit and think of how I could do it. Would I take an overdose, or walk in front of a train, or simply cut my wrists? I am a person who cannot even handle the thought of having an injection and even though they all sounded so painful, I still seriously contemplated taking my own life.

"God help me please," were words I prayed constantly during this time. There was a part of me that wished to be dead so that others could finally see the depths of the pain that I was experiencing, but there was also another part of me that wondered what the Lord, my son, and my family would say and how they would feel if I went ahead with these plans.

In the end I think it was the fact that I knew it was not the Lord's will for me to commit suicide that kept me from actually carrying it out. And I also knew in my heart that I could not do this to my son because he did not deserve it, and I kept wondering, who would care for him the way that I do if I went ahead with these plans?

I did eventually overcome the urges to commit suicide, but the fact still remains, that I did contemplate suicide on many occasions.

- *My confidence was shattered so I dressed up for attention - thinking that this would make me feel good about myself and even to win him back.*

My confidence was another issue that I struggled with. I am generally very confident, and a leader-type of person, but this changed when my relationship ended and he started to see someone else. My confidence was shattered and my self-esteem dropped to an all-time low.

As I mentioned before, I began to feel very ugly both inside and out. So I decided that in a feeble attempt to cheer myself up and feel good about myself I would dress up to look extra special and sexy. There was nothing wrong with this line of action to a certain extent, apart from my motives. My motives were to get attention from male admirers, including my ex, so that I would feel better about myself.

I have always presented myself in an attractive way when it comes to dressing up and making myself look nice and smart, but I was now doing this with the sole intention of making myself look sexier and appealing to the opposite sex. My skirts and dresses got shorter, my tops got tighter, and I lost more weight! But it did not matter how well I tried to present myself on the outside, deep down on the inside I felt ugly and I often hated the way I looked.

Now, you have to remember that I was trying to make myself feel good and outwardly it seemed like I had achieved this, but the reality of it all was that it only made me feel worse, and I still hated myself. (Have you ever thought that doing something would make you happy, but after you have actually done it the fact remains that you are not happy? Well, that's how I felt!)

During this time I was still desperate to be back with my ex and would have done almost anything to win him back. I tried almost every avenue I could think of, but my pain just escalated as he continued to do what he was doing and I did not get the reaction from him that I hoped I would get.

- *Then there was the stage when I wanted to be in competition with my ex and find myself a man much better than him . . . Holy Spirit would not allow me to do this and would always discourage me with the words "you are not ready yet, you need time to heal." And the fact that I now wanted a man that loved God more than me narrowed down my chance that I had a great deal.*

After the initial shock of it all, the constant fighting and arguing and reasoning with my ex-partner, I decided to change my tactics. I knew that my ex still loved me and that I could manipulate him to a certain extent, so I decided that I would hurt him in the way that he had hurt me. I decided that it was time for me to move on and get myself another man.

This line of thinking may not have been my sole reason for looking for another man but I think it was the main one. Another reason for my decision included the fact that if I was with someone else I would not be pining for my ex so much and would therefore be more likely to move on and be free of at least some of the pain that I was going through. So, I went half-heartedly into the 'get another man' mode. But, when I would discuss my plans with the Holy Spirit He would tell me straight, "It will not work because you are not ready Sasha."

I was so devastated with the Lord's response to this, as I really believed that this was the answer to my problems and that this could help me. I could just not understand why God wanted me to go through it alone. *Surely God would want me to have a real person that could help me through*, I thought to myself. (I did not understand then God's reasons for saying wait, but I do understand them now.)

Many of us form a relationship with someone else for one wrong reason or another and this can cause more unnecessary distress. The Lord really just wanted to restore me to my complete self and He also wanted to prove His love to me. This may not have happened if I had given someone else the task of bringing me through my storm.

- *I moved from feeling absolute rage when I saw them together and acting out my rage to the complete opposite – being falsely friendly and acting composed . . . so if this was true why did I need to get out of the situation fast in case I erupted or broke down . . . God help me please!*

The man involved in breaking my heart is the father of my child and at that particular time I found this very hard to deal with. The fact that we had a young son together meant that we were constantly in contact. I had to see him whether I felt like it or not, and part of that contact also meant that I had to deal with the painful prospect of bumping into his girlfriend. This happened on many occasions and the only way I could describe the way I felt at this time is 'extreme discomfort'.

In the initial stage the sight of her made me physically sick with rage and anger and as time went on this would shift between rage to being calm and collected at the drop of a hat. I desperately wanted to get over him but it did not seem to be happening for me. "God help me please," were four words that I prayed constantly, like a scratched record.

The emotional roller coaster I was on lasted for years with me trying so desperately to get off the ride. And it was definitely an exhausting experience that I could have done without. I would not wish such an emotional state on my worst enemy!

- *Tried to act the way they expected me to . . . by now it had been a long time (according to them) and I should be coping and getting over it.*

This bullet point relates to the way that others expected me to act or respond in my situation.

While I was going through my experience many were there to offer me advice about the best way to respond to it. "You should . . . you must . . . try and . . . don't do this, don't do that," were some examples of the advice others would give me, but they were not going through it all and definitely could not feel my pain.

I am not saying that their advice was inappropriate or I did not need their advice or encouragement. I am just saying that if I could have clicked my finger and behaved in an appropriate and acceptable manner, I would have. As much as I tried I just didn't seem to have the strength or will power to do what I knew was the right thing. And if I'm honest I don't know how I would even react to it now if it were to happen again, but I would like to think that I would be able to handle it a lot differently.

Since my experience I am now a firm believer of the saying, "You will never really know how you will respond to a situation until you have actually experienced it firsthand," and, "Never say never!"

- *God . . . "Why won't you stop the pain if you love me? . . . It's been years and I can't take no more . . . Please . . . please . . . please" was the only prayer I would pray . . . sometimes it was the only prayer I could pray.*

Now, although I can hear from the Lord and know what it was like to be in His presence, I am not some kind of super-spiritual person that claims to know all things. What I know about the Lord is what I have personally learned and experienced over the years, and I am still learning. I say this because in this bullet point I am talking about the fact that I was struggling to understand the Lord's methods and way of thinking and doing things. As I went through my experience I even found myself struggling with some of the same issues and questions that a non-believer in Christ would more than likely have to deal with.

There was a time when I believed that the more I cried out to the Lord for His help to save me the worse my distress and pain became! For me, it was as if the Lord was taking great pleasure in watching me suffer alone and I really hated how alone I felt during this time.

My thinking and belief at this time was that at least if I had my ex-boyfriend back, or even another boyfriend, I could channel all my effort, time and energy into that and rid myself of my pain and I would not feel so alone. I just could not understand that if the Bible said all these nice things about the Lord delivering His people, why then was He not rescuing me? I wanted an instant fix for my pain, not the long, drawn-out process that the Lord wanted to take me through and I resented Him for this. So like a spoiled child I would cry out to the Lord to quickly take away my pain so that I could have some peace – never once thinking to myself that I was the problem standing in His Way!

- *. . . The only thing that we both enjoyed was the sex – and at times this would be negative.*

When I first wrote this chapter I had not thought about including this bullet point, but the Holy Spirit spoke to me soon after I had finished writing and asked me to go back and share it with you. I do not know why He has requested this of me but I will be obedient and share it with you anyway. I am sure it will help someone.

In this bullet point I was referring to the stage where we were at sexually in our relationship.

From the beginning of this relationship the sexual chemistry was great. It was not something we had to work too much at, there was plenty of it, and I totally loved how he made me feel sexually. It would be fair to say that sex played a big part in our relationship. In fact I would go a little further and say that it played a major part. Even when we couldn't agree on anything else, this was the one thing we could usually agree on.

"So when did it get negative?" I hear someone ask.

It was after we had broken up and he started to see someone else and I still had a strong desire to continue having sex with him. It seems weird to me now, but in my mind at that time, I felt that if I continued to have sex with him I could manipulate the situation to my benefit. I really delighted in the fact that I still had some control over him and I loved having this control. At least, I thought I did, but in reality it was just a false sense of security that I was clinging to.

The control that I thought I had somehow back-fired on me and the more I continued to have sex with him the more I started to resent him. I resented the fact that he was continuing his other relationship even though I was making myself available to him. I resented the fact that I was allowing him to use me, and I resented the fact that after the actual act of sex was over I would feel dirty and empty and even hated myself. Having sex with him became so emotionally painful that I was no longer in control of the situation or my emotions.

Can you imagine having sex with someone and hoping that it would make you feel good, but after it is all over and done you are left lying there feeling emotional pain and hatred towards the person that you have just given yourself to? Well, this is how I felt and it was terrible! The longer I continued having sex with him the more I hated and resented him but something in me could not stop. It was like the desire had taken over my whole being and was preventing me from making a half-sensible decision.

Again, not everyone will understand here what I was going through. This is one of those things that you will only really understand if you have been through or are going through it, but it is actually a real struggle that many of us deal with. When I look back I know that only the Lord could have gotten me past this barrier and I thank Him that He did it for me, and He will do it for you too!

A Prayer of Encouragement

I pray that the Holy Spirit will help everyone who reads these words to come to a place of peace, where their trust is totally in the Lord. I ask You Lord to deliver them from what others say about them and help them to focus only on what You have to say about them.

I pray that those who are listening to the voices around them will be able to filter out those that are not the voice of God and recognise them for what they really are, distractions of the devil. I also pray that you will yield yourselves to the Lord so that He can do whatever work is necessary in order to free you and restore you to your full potential and glory in Christ Jesus.

I pray this in Jesus' name. **Amen**

Chapter Four

It hurts so bad . . . but I can't let go Lord!

In this chapter I intend to share my personal experiences concerning the issues that I encountered on my journey from pain to freedom — the issues that kept me in bondage for so long — those things that tried so desperately to destroy my life. I am also going to share some of the reasons why I believe some women, and maybe even men, choose to hold on to relationships when they can undeniably see and feel that the relationship is hurting and sometimes even killing them!

I believe that writing this chapter is probably going to be one of the most challenging experiences I will ever have to face, as it means that I will have to revisit some of those things that I tried so hard to justify and forget. And I will have to simply tell them how they really were, without the packaging. You know the packaging I am talking about, the one that we all use to cover things up so nicely, the packaging that we use to conceal what is really in our box, and the packaging that looks so appealing to others.

For me, this is one of those many moments when I am simply going to trust the Lord and let Him guide me through the process. It is one of those moments when I know that the Lord is requesting a sacrifice from me like He did of Abraham in Genesis, Chapter 22. It is one of those moments when I do not know what the Lord will do next, but I have to trust Him to make things known to me in His own perfect time.

My overall motives for writing this book are to first glorify the Lord in my life by declaring to others what He has done for me, and second, to help women, and maybe even men, to overcome their broken hearts and receive their healing. So in order to help you recognise and come to terms with some of the issues that you may be facing in your own situation, I am going to be very open and share with you my own reasons for holding on to my unhealthy relationship against my better judgement. My intention for doing this is so that you will be able to identify with some of my struggles and know that you are not the only one going through such trials. I want you to know that Christians too struggle with real life issues.

To be honest with you, in my opinion, the only real difference between a believer going through such issues and a non-believer is that *"I (the believer) have strength for all things in Christ who empowers me [I am ready for anything and equal to anything through Him who infuses inner strength into me; I am self-sufficient in Christ's sufficiency]"* Philippians 4:13 (AMP, emphasis added). Other than this assurance in Jesus Christ for the believer, we all are destined to experience the same kind of struggles and hardships because nothing we go through is unique to any one particular person (*see 1 Peter 5:9*).

There are some things we just know!

In my own situation I knew that this was not the sort of relationship that I wanted for myself. No, let me start again! By the time I made the rash decision to bail out of my relationship, I knew deep in my heart that this was not the kind of relationship I wanted to be in.

Although I felt this way, and had been feeling like this for awhile, it was one of the most upsetting decisions that I have ever had to make. Even now, at the time of writing this book, almost ten years later I am still not completely convinced that I made the right decision back then. And at the time of writing theses words, I still have to ask the Holy Spirit to help me come to terms with my decision to end that relationship because I still have a lot of love for my first love. Looking back on the whole episode, even with the knowledge and understanding I have now, if I am totally honest with you I would have probably stayed in that relationship if I could have turned back time. On the other hand in my heart I really do believe that this relationship was dying and had to end.

"So why could I not simply end it and move on with my life?"

That is a question that I have asked myself for years and I will open up and share with you some of my main reasons for hanging in there for so long, even after the pain became unbearable!

As the years have passed, I often thought about and asked the Holy Spirit to help me understand why I stayed in the wilderness for so long, like the children of Israel in the book of Exodus. When I say the wilderness, I mean why did I continue to stay in such a dry place for years when I could obviously see that this kind of relationship was not helpful to me. (I talk about it now with much insight, understanding, and wisdom, but let the truth be known that as I travelled through my valley, this was far from the case.)

As you read through the reasons that kept me confused, unable to think clearly, and holding on even when it was hurting me, I want you to take note and ask the Holy Spirit to reveal to you the things that you may be holding on to. I also want you to ask Him to help you let go, especially if you have come to the point when you know deep down that it is time to do so.

I know — even the thought of this can be hard to swallow, but you're going to be alright!

Familiarity, cycles and patterns!

Familiarity and learnt cycles and patterns were probably one of my biggest reasons for holding on to my relationship when things got unpleasant and began to hurt. As I mentioned before, I had known this man from a very young age. He was the first man that I had ever loved and I had grown to trust him with my life.

74

During the time we spent together, he had somehow proven himself trustworthy. He had loved on me, he made a lot of sacrifices for me, and he guided me through situations that I was not experienced in. He had pampered me and invested a lot of time and effort in me. This man even permed and washed my hair for me — I could go on forever detailing every nice thing this man ever did for me.

From the day we met and got together, he showed me nothing but love and respect. This, of course, in turn made it extremely easy for me to fall head over heels in love with him, even at a time when I was not really looking for a boyfriend or love. As we grew closer we became inseparable and familiar with one another. I began to know what he liked and disliked and he learned the same about me. There were literally times where we would spend days wrapped in each other's company, laughing, loving, staring, holding, playing, listening to music, watching television, smoking, and so on.

The fact that we were so into each other meant that we became totally comfortable with one another and this in turn led to a sense of familiarity. We became so familiar with each other! We became familiar with certain patterns, familiar with the way we liked things and familiar with each other's families.

There was nothing wrong with this familiarity in itself, except that it eventually led to a false sense of trust. Even when we would argue and fight it did not cross my mind that I would ever have to deal with the worst-case scenario of what would happen to me if the relationship were to end?

So when the relationship did in fact come to an end, the familiarity and the cycle of breaking up and getting back together again made it almost impossible for me to really comprehend and believe that the relationship had indeed ended and that he had moved on and was with someone else. My mind could not seem to comprehend that the relationship was over and this kept me holding on in the hope that everything would somehow work itself out. But how wrong I was in all of my thinking, wishing, and reasoning!

Emotions!

The subject of emotions is something we can all relate to, right? We all experience most of the same emotions at some point in our lives so we know fully well what they feel like and how they may make us react in a given situation.

If I were to say that my emotions did not play a prominent role in my situation, I would be telling an outright lie; my emotions controlled everything! My emotions controlled all of my actions, how I would react to things, and I would even go as far as to say they controlled my life.

I have always been an emotional person and I can swing from one emotion to another quite easily if I allow myself to. But after my relationship ended I became an instant emotional wreck. I would go from happy to sad, calm to hysterical, chirpy to depressed, expressing love to expressing hatred, and tears to smiles at the slightest image or thought in my mind. It would be more than fair to say that during this season of my life I lost complete control of my emotions and that they were now dominating all my actions. My emotions had become my master and dictator!

My emotions would determine how I would feel on a particular day, they would tell me what I needed, they would tell me what I needed to hear and even how I was to behave in a particular situation. They controlled everything about me, including my decisions and in some cases my lack of decision making.

Being emotional and having to deal with a whirlwind of events all at the same time, will more than likely affect your ability to make level-headed decisions, as was the case with me. And likewise, being heart-broken, in pain, and having to deal with all of these things at the same time made it almost impossible for me to make rational decisions. In my state of weakness and depression, I chose to allow my emotions to determine my actions and the course that I followed.

I knew that my pathetic decision to continue to hold on to this person even when he had let go of me was foolish, but at the same time it still somehow seemed like it was the best course of action. The Holy Spirit would say to me all the time, "Sasha let go . . . it will be for your own good . . . trust Me," but I would just think of Him as crazy for even suggesting this to me. I honestly did not find the Holy Spirit's advice useful at all, and my response to Him would be, "Lord, how can you even ask this of me? Can you not see how I am feeling as a result of not having this person? Do you even care Lord, because if you did care you would never ask this of me?" The whole thing was a battle and this fight continued until the Holy Spirit eventually taught me how to gain control of and manage my emotions.

In my spirit I suspect that getting control of your emotions is probably one of the main issues that you and most people reading this book are struggling with. So I am really happy that I decided to go with the Lord on this one, and include this issue.

Emotions are a good thing to have and we cannot possibly function without them, but the Lord intended for us to be in control of them. There must be a balance! It is only in having this balance that we can find the strength we need to overcome our trials.

It took me years to conquer this battle and in the period in-between I simply continued to fight my emotional battle in my own strength to no avail. And the reason I chose not to listen to the Holy Spirit's sound advice was because I did not believe that He could help me.

When I look back at the time that I spent battling with my emotions, I now realise that I did not do myself any favours by being disobedient to the Holy Spirit. I thought I could help myself, but instead I made my situation worse!

Keeping up appearances!

Keeping up appearances is a stronghold that can keep you in bondage all your life if you give in to it. It can even change the whole course of your destiny. It is a very serious matter and you are going to have to get control of it and make sure it does not govern your life. Many of us spend years and sometimes even our entire lives perfecting our "face masks" so that we can portray them to the rest of the world.

This facade is one of those things that you learn from the beginning of your life, and it is usually influenced largely by your parents and immediate family. From a young age I can remember being told by my mum, "Don't chat about my business to anyone," and thinking to myself, "But the thing that she is telling me not to talk about is actually my business and about me." Nevertheless I learned very quickly not to share certain things and what was acceptable to share with others. After awhile it was like an unsaid rule that you knew to comply with, and I just got on with it.

As a result of this mindset, when I encountered my drama and was going through such a distressing time I became absolutely worried at the prospect of others seeing and knowing what I was really going through. I had always been strong and I still wanted others to see me as strong, so the fact that this guard was slipping really made me feel vulnerable. I do not really know why I felt this way, but I guess it had a lot to do with some of the learned behaviour patterns and attitudes I was exposed to as a child.

I went through my season of heartbreak and distress desperately trying to convince the outside world that my circumstances were not affecting me, when the real truth was that they were slowly killing me. It was all so hard, so draining and so fake, but I had been taught so well and I could not let myself slip just because I was experiencing a little pressure. (This was basically what I used to tell myself as I put on my masks to greet the world.)

Now, before I share with you some of the various masks that I used to wear, and you will probably be familiar with some of these, I want to first tell you that there are many different masks available and the masks that we choose for ourselves will often be influenced by the people that we have around us or by the situations that we are in. I know this because I had different masks to greet the various groups and individuals involved in my life. This was definitely a time when I found it hard just being me!

When I was around my mum and my family I wore the mask that portrayed the facade, "I am hurt and going through some things, but it is not that bad . . . really I am alright." I wore this mask because I knew that it would upset my family to see me really down in the dumps, and I knew that they could not help the way I was feeling, even if they wanted to.

There was the mask that I wore for my son that portrayed a strong, caring, loving, and fun mother. I had no choice but to wear this one around him because he was very young and did not understand in the slightest what was going on concerning his dad and me.

There was the mask that I wore for the man that had broken my heart which portrayed the image that I was coping well despite the circumstances. I wore this mask for him because I knew that he found weak women very unattractive and I would have done anything to keep his love and favour.

There was the mask that I wore for his family. This mask was very difficult to wear because it was one of confusion. When I say confusion, I am talking about the confusion of knowing that they sincerely loved and cared for me but at the same time feeling some uncertainty of that fact. At the time this confusion stemmed from my thought of: *How could they love and care about me and still love and care about the woman who is helping to cause me so much pain?* I just could not understand this and my actions and behaviour towards some of his family members really reflected this confusion.

There was the mask that I wore for the 'other woman'. It was one that said, "You may have my man, but I know you do not have his heart and because of this I delight in the fact that I am a worry to you and I will keep on being a worry to you until you cannot take anymore."

(Yes, I know it sounds un-godly like and bitchy, but I am just being honest with you.)

And finally, there was the mask that I wore for my friends and the rest of the outside world. This one was the hardest mask to wear because it was the one that I had to put on most often. This mask had to portray my usual strong character that everyone loved to be around, the one who was always totally on top of things and knew how to have fun, the one who knew how to get what she wanted when she wanted it, and the one who could make people laugh.

My Lord, it was so hard dressing up with all these masks while at the same time trying to nurse my broken heart in silence. And to be honest I do not know how I coped with it all but by the grace and mercy of God.

Keeping up appearances for the world's sake prevented me from moving on and experiencing the freedom I longed for. It is not worth your time and effort and no one will ever thank you for doing it. For these reasons I challenge you today to ask the Holy Spirit to help you identify your own masks and hang them up for good.

Sex and soul ties!

While thinking about the right words to use to explain each of the reasons why I kept holding on to this unhealthy relationship, I have experienced a few challenges. It is not that I do not know what I am trying to say or anything like that, but it is more a case of really wanting to explain myself clearly to you in a way that you can identify with and relate to.

I had initially put them in order of the ones I wanted to discuss first but for some reason, as I asked the Holy Spirit to help me with my writer's block, the words concerning this area seemed to readily flow out onto the page. (I actually wrote this section first.)

I know a lot of you are familiar with the subject of sex, but I sense in my spirit that there are a few of you asking, "What is a soul tie?" So I will try and explain to you what my understanding of a soul tie is in the simplest terms. I have read a few books on the subject matter for my own knowledge and understanding, but I am not really an expert on it, so for this reason I will only share with you my personal understanding of it. It may be helpful for you, if you are not familiar with this subject matter, to research it for yourselves. You will definitely be blessed by obtaining such knowledge and it will help you understand the whole issue of soul ties a lot better.

Basically a soul tie is a spiritual connection between two or more people. It literally means that your souls have been connected to one another because you have allowed them to be entwined with one another. It happens when your soul — your will, your intellect, your mind, your body and your emotions — is spiritually tied and connected together, whether you like it or not, and whether you believe it or not. I know what I am saying may seem quite deep, but it is true. (Like I said before, if you are not familiar with the subject of soul ties, I really do encourage you to go and study the subject matter for yourself.)

I was once given an audio tape on the subject of soul ties by a friend. The man of God speaking had obviously studied this subject area, with the help of the Holy Spirit, and made some statements to the effect that, when two unmarried people are involved sexually, they enter into a false covenant agreement with one another and their souls are spiritually tied. He explained that this meant that spiritually speaking, they have entered into an illegal marriage. The marriage is illegal in the sense that it is not recognised by God and is not part of His will, because an actual legal commitment to one another has not been made. I know the whole world is having pre-marital sex and it is very much accepted in our society today, but it is still not acceptable to God and His Word never changes *(see Isaiah 40:8)*.

To some of you, the fact that you have entered into an illegal marriage may seem like a great thing — it did to me! But if you are trying to end, or have been forced to end, a relationship, it can become very emotionally challenging and extremely draining.

As a young Christian I did not read or study my Bible that much, as I did not feel that I needed to. I believed that I had everything in my life under control and my relationship with the Lord would simply be a tool I would use to get things that I could not get on my own. Basically, I invited Jesus Christ into my heart a few years into this particular relationship as a tool to help me keep my man, and at the time this was my sole intention for accepting the Lord. But as I began to familiarize myself with the Bible and listen to Godly wisdom and counsel, I became aware of the fact that it was not the Lord's will for me to have sex with someone that I was not married to. So this is what I did: I blocked out that part of the Bible and counsel and made justifications to the effect of, *it is alright . . . the guy I am having sex with is my baby's father, God understands*, and so on. And I did this for no other reason than the fact that I loved having sex with this person, loved the feeling of enjoyment and pleasure it gave me, and I was not prepared to give him or it up for anyone. Even if the Lord had manifested Himself right there in front of me and told me to stop it, I would not have given up my desire to have sex with this guy. I just loved it!

These feelings and desires carried on for years and sex became like an addiction to me. I was addicted to the point where I now hated the person that I was having sex with, yet I still could not control or stop myself. I was addicted to the false sense of security that having sex with this person gave me, just like a drug user is addicted to cocaine or heroine!

Now, like I said before, I continued to have sex with this man, even after he had started a new relationship. I did this because my mind would tell me that I had a right to continue to have sex with him because I had known him before his present partner and he was the father of my child. It would tell me that if I stopped having sex with him he would definitely not come back to me because that sexual connection would no longer be there. My mind would tell me that if I continued to have sex with him, I could control and manipulate him into doing what I wanted him to do. It would tell me that I could use it as a weapon to get back at him if he ever got me angry and I wanted to hurt him in return for the way I believed he had hurt me. It told me that I could not possibly live without this person and that no one else would ever make me feel like he did sexually. My mind would even fantasize and play video images about sexual encounters with this person on a daily basis.

I battled with these thoughts and feelings for years, not realizing that it could have been much easier for me if I just made the decision to confront, repent, and deal with my sin and actions. (It is easy to say all this now that I have been through the fire and come out the other side, but in all fairness, it is a hard decision to make when you are actually going through it.)

My point is that my desire and addiction to sex with this man contributed largely to my pain and to the reasons why I could not let go and move on with my life. Of course, I did not think this at the time because I was so "*in love*" with this man, but I now know for a fact that this is the case.

When I did eventually relent and cry out to the Lord for help with this issue, He revealed to me the error of my ways and helped me to conquer it. I tried for years to conquer my battle with fornication but could not overcome it, and it was not until I confessed my sin and started to trust and obey the Lord that He was able to intervene. And after the Holy Spirit helped me to control my flesh, I became spiritually, emotionally and physically stronger and wiser.

I am not naïve and I know that many of us struggle tremendously with this area. From personal experience I know that this is not an easy area to conquer. But I also know that as long as you give in to this desire or addiction you will always be asking the question, "God, why can't I let go?"

Loneliness!

Loneliness! At some point or another in our lives we have all had to deal with this feeling, reality, or state of mind. There are times when we look forward to being on our own, and there are other times when we dislike the fact that we are alone — it all depends on the needs or desires of each individual.

I am a person that enjoys being on my own most of the time, like when I am listening to music or seeking God's presence. But there are indeed times when I don't want to be alone and enjoy the company of other people. To be honest with you, it all depends on how I am feeling and my mood.

One thing I am sure of is that I do not like the thought of having to be on my own because someone else has forced me into solitude. If you can relate to this kind of thinking, you will probably understand when I say that I did not like it when my boyfriend of almost seven years decided to leave me devastated and alone. It was not a place I wished to be and when it happened it came so unexpectedly.

The day I found out that my ex-boyfriend had started a new relationship was the moment great feelings of loneliness hit me and began to consume and eat me up. Even when I was in the company of others, I still could not shake off the feeling of loneliness.

Can you believe that I even felt lonely when this man was physically holding me in his arms?

Let us stop here to create in your mind a picture of my last comment. My ex-boyfriend would come to my home to see my son or me and somehow I would manage to seduce or manipulate him into having sex with me, but would still be left in a state of aloneness. There were even times that he would spend the whole night over at my flat and we would be in each other's company the whole night, but I would still feel like I was alone!

At the time I could not fully understand why I was feeling like this, but I now know that it was because only the Lord could fill the hunger and quench the thirst of my mind, body and soul (*see John 6:35*).

Fear!

Fear can be one of the most faithful friends that you will ever have. If you let it, fear will stick to you like a stamp to a letter. Do you know that most of us live our entire lives with some kind of fear, although the Bible tells us in 2 Timothy 1:7 that *"God has not given us a spirit of fear; but of power, and love and of a sound mind."* But, I guess if you do not read the Word of God or believe in its authenticity, some type of fear will always intimidate you.

One of the main reasons I held on to this relationship long after it ended and started to hurt me was my fear of experiencing the unknown. I was absolutely terrified at the prospect of having to move on and try something new. My mind would not let me, especially when part of this meant that I would inevitably have to be with someone else. At the time, even the thought of this made me physically sick and extremely uncomfortable.

I mentioned before in a previous chapter that I had to deal with my fear of seeing my ex-partner intimate with someone else, and this fear was probably the most heart-breaking one of all. But apart from this major fear, I also had others to deal with. There was the fear that if I gave myself to someone else my ex would never want me back, the fear of my ex giving his heart away to someone else, the fear of having to face people, the fear of always feeling like this, the fear of actually dying of my pain, the fear of being on my own, the fear of completely letting go, the fear of having my ex in my life forever because of our son and the fear that I would never find a cure for my broken heart. *Gosh, the fears were endless!*

My fears were not only endless. They also gripped my heart in such a way that I was unable to think straight, sleep at night, eat food, and generally care about any of the others things that were going on in my life. It was awful!

Lack of self esteem and self worth!

If a close friend or relative was to use words to describe me before this time, "confident" would have definitely been among those used. From a very young age I was always the one that would stand out in the crowd because of this characteristic. I had the natural ability and confidence to go after what I wanted, and I would usually get it. Whether it is the confidence to get or do something negative or positive, the fact still remains the same: I was a very confident and strong-willed person.

But if this was really the case, how then did I go so quickly from having such great confidence and high self-esteem to a place where I was left struggling with issues such as lack of self-esteem and very low confidence?

Well the truth is that I do not know how I made this transition, but one thing I do know is that it happened quite quickly and drastically. My relationship with this man had ended and as a result I took it very badly. And before I knew it my self-esteem and self-worth were at an all-time low — as quick as that!

The rejection I felt had a tremendous affect on me because I had adored my ex and held his opinion of me so highly for so many years. I had loved this man so much that I would think highly of everything he said to or about me. I respected him so much that I would have done almost anything that he had asked me to do, even if it meant laying down my own needs, desires, and goals in order to do so. The bottom line was that I cared more about what he said or thought about me than I cared or thought about myself. *Not a wise move!*

Now, if you are at this point or you have been there before, you will be familiar with some of the negative things that the mind begins to tell you at a time like this. You know, the things such as: *If you really loved him the way you said you did, why then did you not treat him right? A real woman would know how to treat her man. The woman he is with now seems like a much better woman than you are. Will I ever be able to have another relationship again? There must be something wrong with me for him to say that he still loves me, yet does not want to be with me.* And, *You may be an attractive woman that other men seem to comment about and desire to be with, but this does not really matter when the man you love is prepared to let you go!* Well I endured all these thoughts and feelings for years.

Eventually, if you keep meditating on such things they will begin to wear you down. And this is what happened to me: my self-esteem and self-worth hit rock bottom and I lost all my self-confidence!

When you are experiencing low self-esteem and self-worth you may begin to look upon the opinions and words of others as the gospel truth, and this is what I did. I could not think or feel for myself so I continued to crave and hold on to my ex's perception of me. When he would treat me nicely and say nice things to me my self-esteem and confidence would be high and I would feel good about myself. But when he would attack me with cruel words, views and opinions, my self-esteem, self confidence and self-worth would slump right back down again.

I was in a place where I was feeling so weak from my pain that I could not even find the strength I needed to pick myself up. So I thought to myself that it would be much better for me and my sanity if I continued to hold on and wait for him to pick me up and make me feel good about myself whenever he chose or wanted to.

Again, to some of you reading my reasons for holding on may sound silly, but like I keep saying, you have to experience it to understand the stuff that comes with it!

Ego and Selfishness!

In the opening section of this chapter I acknowledged the fact that my reasons for holding on and your reasons for holding on may not be exactly the same. However, for some reason I think that this next reason, selfishness and ego, is going to be one of those issues that is the same for everyone.

We all have a tendency to be selfish and to think of ourselves first and to be honest, even with the help of the Holy Spirit I still find myself dealing with this issue on a regular basis.

When my relationship ended, my mind could not seem to handle the thought that this man had moved on so quickly. In Chapter One I shared with you that the final break up was instigated by me because I was not really happy with the direction this relationship was going in. I had called for the end of this relationship but did not really think it would be the final end.

To be honest with you, I would probably have been much happier to accept the break-up and move on quite peacefully if it was on my terms, but when he switched the script on me and started seeing someone else it was a big blow to my ego. I was selfish in that I wanted the outcome to be on my terms and the fact that he now seemed to be the one in control of the situation was devastating to me.

My selfishness did not stop there. After we split I selfishly decided that I would do everything in my power to keep him confused and unable to move on properly with his new girlfriend. (Gosh, when I look back I was so ruthless in my attitude and behaviour and I did not really care about anyone or anything other than myself.)

My selfishness and egocentric attitudes and actions were one of my many reasons for holding on and again, they were contributing to my pain and I did not even realise it until the Holy Spirit began to show me this.

. . . just tricks of the enemy!

Our individual reasons for holding on to a relationship that has gone sour may differ, and in some aspects they may even reflect the same aspects as the next person. Your experience may even seem a million times worse than mine. And on the other hand another person may say, "Well, at least I have not got it as bad as she had it." Everyone is different and will go through their own individual personal experiences, but one thing I am very sure of is that most negative things that we as human beings go through are simply tricks of the devil.

Sometimes we do not have a choice in the things that life throws at us but we can choose what we are going to believe as we go through them.

Most of us are not familiar with the Bible and do not know the everlasting hope we can experience if we just get familiar with it. I once watched a film that gave an acronym for the word "Bible" as "**B**asic **I**nstructions **B**efore **L**eaving **E**arth" and my spirit jumped on it straight away. For me this acronym summed it up in simple terms God's purpose for giving us the Bible. And to be honest with you it is so true.

In the Bible, in John 10:10, Jesus speaks about the devil's main intentions for God's people. Basically, the devil's work is to try to steal, kill, and destroy us. And I am sure you would agree with me when I say that he is really dedicated to enforcing his authority, and very good at his job.

Now listen to the best part of this same verse. Jesus ended it by saying that His purpose for coming was to give us a rich and satisfying, abundant life. *Everyone say thank God for Jesus!*

To those of us experiencing some kind of hardship, these words can be so comforting and reassuring, but the devil can prey on the ignorance of someone that has never heard of or seen these words before. The devil tries to trick them into believing that what they are experiencing and going through will lead to the point of destruction. Like I said before, he thrives on trickery!

This is even evident in the story of Adam and Eve's fall *(see Genesis 3)*. Many of us are familiar with this story, but for those of you who are not I will give you a short summary of it.

In Genesis Chapter 2, God creates Adam and gives him a warning not to eat from the "tree of the knowledge of good and evil," a simple instruction, right! God then gives Adam a woman called Eve and the two of them live happily together until one day the devil, disguised as a serpent, asks Eve the question, "Did God really say you must not eat the fruit from any of the trees in the garden?"

This was Eve's first mistake — she listened! And when you start to listen to some of the suggestions in your mind, would you agree that this is probably the moment when things first start to go downhill for you in your life?

Now, because the devil got Eve to listen to him and eventually converse with him, he was now in a place where he could make some seemingly logical suggestions to her like, "Of course you will not die," and, "God just does not want you to become as powerful as Him."

By that point the devil is well on his way to tricking Adam and Eve into doubting what God, their creator, had told them and warned them against. I know it is unbelievable right, and I often hear people say things like, "How could they have been so stupid?" Or, "If it was me I would have . . ." But would we or could we have really done it any better? I don't think so. The truth is that in many situations the devil is tricking us left, right, and centre, and many of us are bowing down to his suggestions and trickery and do not even know it.

I sense that someone may be confused by this comment. So, let's take me as an example. I knew the Word of God and His will for me. I knew how to hear the voice of God, I had experienced His awesome presence and power, but even after all that I still allowed the devil to trick me into doubting the Lord for years!

When you are experiencing something so painful or distressing many of the negative thoughts or suggestions come from a main source — the devil. You will need to recognise them and choose not to accept them. Here is a suggestion: replace every negative suggestion with a positive suggestion or Word from the Lord. They can be found throughout the Bible. Or you can just simply take time to thank the Lord that you have your eyes to see and air to breathe!

As we come to the end of this chapter I hope that my main reasons for holding on to my relationship have blessed you in some way. They may not totally reflect what you are actually dealing with or have had to deal with but the core fact is still the same: whatever your reasoning, we all still choose to hold on.

I want you to be honest with yourself and ask the Holy Spirit to reveal to you what and why you may be choosing to hold on against your better judgement. Let's face it, you would not have been attracted to this book if you did not need some answers for your pain and heartbreak, so just be honest with yourself and ask the Holy Spirit to help you to recognise, get control over, and let go of all these barriers preventing you from moving on.

Let us pray!

Holy Spirit, I ask that as I share my heart and soul for You, You will move in my life and the lives of those that You desire to touch and help through my words.

Continue to help me to seek after You and Your presence; for it is in this secret place that I am safe and have found freedom (Psalm 91). Continue to break me Lord! Continue to mould me Lord! Continue to make me more and more like You in everything that I do and say.

I pray that every reader of these words will open up and share more with You. I pray that they will learn to be honest with You and themselves, as You begin to peel off their 'packaging.' And finally, I pray that they will receive their freedom from every stronghold that threatens to destroy their lives. I ask this in Jesus' name,

Amen.

Chapter Five

Please help me someone . . . anyone . . . anything . . . !

In this chapter I am going to talk about the subject of looking for help in all the wrong places. These are places that you hope will help you to ease and eliminate your pain but you soon realise they won't.

In my desperate attempt to rid myself of my constant torment, I would run to and fro between places that I believed would help eliminate my pain only to find that they did not work for me. I am going to revisit some of the places that I anxiously searched, desperately looking for help and deliverance — the places where I could not seem to find any hope or peace.

Looking for help is something we all do when we are faced with a desperate struggle or situation and if we are not too careful the places we choose to run to may contribute significantly to the pain we are already experiencing.

This was, of course, the case with me! I spent years running between dry, fruitless places that could only give me a short-term fix and relief from my pain, and despite this fact I was true to those short-term fixes, as an addict is to his addiction. And the funny thing was that even when I knew better, I still kept on going back to check out these places hoping that they would have somehow acquired an answer to my problems. Even when I had the Holy Spirit's help at hand and He was providing me with all the right solutions and answers for my problems, I still felt the need to return to these places to see if they could offer me a better and quicker fix than the one that the Lord was offering.

Don't get me wrong, I was very grateful to the Lord for the comfort and assurance that He gave me, but was He giving me the answers that my heart and soul so desperately wanted to hear?

If you are wondering what the answer is to that question the answer is no, the Holy Spirit did not give me the answers that I really wanted to hear at that time! It did not matter how many tears I cried or how much I acted like a spoiled child that could not get her own way, the Holy Spirit still did not give in to my tantrums.

During this tough time the Lord's reasons for not giving in to me were way beyond my level of understanding and very painful to deal with. I just could not understand why He was taking so long to cut off my pain supply.

When I think back on this experience, the whole prolonged process was like waiting to have one of those painful injections that is needed to safeguard you from catching a disease: although you know that it will be good for you in the long run you just can't get away from that simple little fact that it is going to hurt you when you receive it.

I realise that for some of you this metaphor may not seem painful at all but for those of you who are like me and get extremely apprehensive and terrified at the thought of having an injection, you can probably appreciate my comparison.

For years I struggled to understand why the Lord, with all His wisdom and knowledge, would refuse to give in to "my great plan." Surely I knew myself better than anyone else, including Him, and if He would just follow my great ideas concerning my situation, I thought that I would be freed of every bit of pain that I was experiencing. But I was just kidding myself! It took the Holy Spirit ages to convince me that my way could not work and He also shared with me, on many occasions, why He was not going to give in to my tantrums and demands. I regularly fought this same old battle with the Holy Spirit for years, until somehow He eventually persuaded me that His Way was the only way *(see Deuteronomy 10:12)*.

The Holy Spirit had to take me through a humbling process where I would have no choice but to surrender it all to Him. And I will be the first to admit that this process was extremely difficult and uncomfortable for me. It required me to let go of all those beliefs, things, people, thoughts, and ideas that I held on to so dearly and forced me to cling to Him alone.

In the short time that you have been reading this chapter, some of you may probably be asking yourself questions such as, "Do I really want to stop searching in these places? Am I really ready to trust and surrender all to the Lord? Lord, I know that You do not normally permit Your children to do it their own way, but can You just do this one little thing for me?" I know this because I also asked the Lord and myself questions like this in my desperate fight to overcome my heart-break and pain.

As you continue to read on, it may seem to you like I do not have the answers and solutions to your personal struggles but I can assure you, the Holy Spirit has them all and He will meet you at the point of your need.

Now, come with me as I share with you some of those places that I travelled through on my journey — the places which gave me a false sense of hope and security, the dry, fruitless places, the places where many of us tend to run to in our search for a way out of our distress, pain, and depression.

I searched in a place called sex

Before we explore this place, I would first like to share with you my attitude towards sex before the start of this relationship.

As early as my teenage years, I knew that I was not going to be one of those girls who slept around. I was quite shy in this sense and quite protective of my body, and to be honest with you, I was not really interested in having a boyfriend or a sexual relationship. (At the time I would say that I was more interested in having a laugh and fun with my friends at school than I was with being in a relationship.)

Many of my friends started having sexual relationships before I did. And although I did feel some peer pressure to catch up with them I could take it or leave it — I wasn't fussed.

Although I did experience some peer pressure to start a sexual relationship, I had always decided that the person that I would choose to have a sexual relationship with would be my boyfriend and not just anybody.

In my last statement you'll notice that I said my boyfriend and not my husband. And I realise that some people maybe shocked by this, so let me explain myself. I did not use the term 'husband' because I had determined in my mind from a young teenager that I would never get married. (The state of all the ones around me at this time helped me to come to this decision.) Although I had attended a Catholic secondary school and church, I did not know God's views on the subject of sex outside of marriage and I did not wish to know them. All I knew was that I wanted to have a sexual relationship with someone that I trusted and not someone who would use me and then throw me aside.

By the time I had met my then-boyfriend I had already envisioned in my mind the type of boyfriend I wanted to have. He would have to be handsome, kind, and trustworthy. (I know you're probably thinking to yourself, "You really sold yourself short, girl," but what can I say, I was only fifteen at the time.) So when my ex-boyfriend first came into my life it wasn't hard for him to tick all my boxes. He was kind, handsome, and trustworthy, and while the relationship was going well and everything was gravy, so to speak, I grew to trust this man wholeheartedly with my mind, body, and soul.

My ultimate desire was for someone to love me for me. I wanted unconditional love, but what I did not know was that humans are incapable of giving or receiving such love without the help of the Lord.

It is simple. You cannot give what you do not know and you cannot really know what you do not have!

It is only as a result of my growing relationship with the Lord that I have been able to experience such love and I now have some understanding of how I could possibly show someone else unconditional love *(see I Corinthians 13)*. But isn't it funny how at a time when I desperately craved unconditional love from this person I was not in a position to give it back to him?

Now let us get back to the matter of searching for help and deliverance in the place called sex. To put it in simple terms, sex was never my main desire for forming my relationship with this man. Really, I just wanted someone to love me for me and not for what he could physically get from me.

Before this relationship sex was not something of great relevance and importance to me — I could take it or leave it. But, after I had actually experienced sex, it was a whole new ball game. It was as though a whole new world of emotions and possibilities had opened up for me, and I loved every moment of it!

Now, taking into consideration all that I have just shared with you in this section concerning my attitude towards sex and saving myself for the "right" person, you would have thought that when my boyfriend broke the trust that I had built up in him I would naturally stop having sex with him straight away, right?

Well we all know that it did not happen like this and that I kept on exploring that same old dry place called sex over and over and over again. I spent a lot of time searching through this place in the hope of finding answers for my pain and troubles, but it was a complete waste of my time. My pain and troubles just seemed to get worse as the months and years went by.

It even got to a point where I would find myself waiting desperately for him to come over to my flat just to see if he could help take me back to that sexual place, the place where I had learned to feel so safe and secure with him. I would find myself desperately looking for the same old feelings and sense of security that having sex with this man had initially given me in the good old days, when the truth was that they were not there anymore. For some strange reason I just could not seem to understand where they had gone and why they were no longer there. I could not get it into my head that those days were over and they were never going to return. Although I knew that my deepest feelings for him had gone soon after he started his other relationship, I still remained searching in this dry place for years.

I may have been in denial over the whole situation but I was not stupid, I knew exactly what I was doing and no one forced me to make the decisions that I made. I may not have had the strength to do it differently at the time, but I knew that what I was doing was not right. The more time I spent reading my Bible and dwelling in the presence of God the more I began to realise that this was not His will for me. But still, this did not seem to deter me! I just did not seem to have the strength or the desire to stop returning to this empty place even after knowing that the Lord loved me more than anyone or anything ever could.

Can you imagine how this made me feel, knowing full well that I was compromising myself and my relationship with God, the Lord, who only ever wanted to help and love me? I felt awful, used, hurt, stupid, rejected, depressed, bitter, hatred, disgust, lonely, ugly, and physically sick to my stomach.

This was definitely a physically, emotionally, and spiritually stressful time for me and my poor judgements and decisions to keep going back to this place only added to my confusion and pain.

I searched in a place called studies and career!

In this next section I intend to share with you how not even my studies and a foreseeable career could help me get rid of my pain and mend my broken heart.

I mentioned before in Chapter One that there were some things that I perceived to be blessings during this dark period of my life. One of these things was the fact that I had taken steps to kick-start my career by enrolling in a college course.

Now the truth is that I did complete this course and go on to graduate from a university course. And I know that this will be viewed by some as being a great achievement considering the circumstances, but I want you to know that these achievements in my studies did not help to ease my pain or heal my broken heart, they just made it bearable. The more I seemed to throw myself into my studies and try to make school the centre of my attention the more I felt empty and frustrated. The more I tried to forget about my personal problems and tell myself, at *least I have my new career to look forward to*, the more I seemed to spiral deeper into a state of depression.

This place called studies and careers that I searched through at this time could not and did not help me deal with the hurt and pain I was experiencing. I would spend hours at college engaged with other people and then go home to spend hours doing my assignments, but my broken heart would still always be there in the background. I could not escape from the fact that my spirit and my heart were severely battered and bruised and it did not matter how much I tried to hide in my studies, the root of my pain could not be relieved.

I went through nearly six years of studies, nursing my broken heart, doing all I knew to do and I can honestly say that my studies did not bring relief to my broken heart. The only thing it helped me do was channel my time and efforts into a good cause. It enabled me to use my time more wisely instead of indulging in my pain twenty-four hours a day, but it did not do what I thought it could do — *it did not heal my broken heart and pain!* After the days had ended and all my assignments were completed I would climb into bed and all the same old feelings of pain and hurt would rush back to bombard my mind and crush my spirit. I would lay there in absolute agony and tears, wondering if the day would ever come when I would be free from all these feelings. I would lay there and listen to all that the devil would share with me, the things like, "It does not matter what you think you are going to be or achieve because you are still going to have this pain in your heart."

The devil used to often make negative suggestions to me and for a long time I continued to believe them over God's Word. I chose to believe the devil's suggestions and lies over God's Word because they seemed more real to me than God's did. At the time the devil's suggestions seemed so real because I could actually see them happening in my life, and it is easier to trust in what you can see, whereas God's Word and suggestions seemed great but I could not quite see how or when I could possibly experience or achieve them.

Again, like my search in the place called sex, this dry place was fruitless. As much as it helped me progress into bigger and better things career-wise, it still could not give me the help that I needed to heal the pain of my broken heart. Only the Lord could give me this healing and restoration for my soul and that is actually what He did when I finally surrendered my will to Him and declared that I would only do things His Way.

I searched in a place called friends and family!

This is an area that I believe we all go to in our desperate search for a way out of our pain and hurt. Family and friends, and in particular "families," are usually a safe haven for us all to run to in our time of need, and to be honest I do not see anything wrong with us doing this. In most cases, from the day you are born your family is there with you, and you can not choose your family — you are stuck with them for life! Family members get the opportunity to grow with you and therefore get to witness all those changes, downfalls, triumphs and highlights of your life, which others may not get to see.

Then there are your friends, the people that you choose for one reason or the other to become part of your life. Some of us have better judgement than others and tend to choose friends that we somehow know will be good for us — friends who we know will be there for us when we need them.

I thank the Lord all the time for my family and real friends because if it were not for their love and support during the harder times, my life would not have been bearable. Some of them have stood by me in desperate times, stood by me in embarrassing times, conversed with me well into the night, gave me useful advice, warned me, and loved me. I would not have been where I am today if the Lord had not used some of my family and friends to support me in my times of need.

The fact that I have started discussing this point in such a way has probably left you wondering why, if family and friends are so great, I would include it in a chapter that is talking about searching in wrong places for your help and deliverance. So let me explain. There is nothing wrong with having family and friends and we should strive to love our family and friends in a way that is pleasing to the Lord *(see Matthew 19:19)*. However, the main point that I want to make clear to you is that we should always put God first in our lives, above and before anything, including our family and friends.

During the time I was going through my distress I did not understand this. I was aware of it, but I did not understand why the Lord would want any of us to put Him first before our own children, husbands, and family. I could not get my head around this concept, and the fact that I could not understand this eventually led to me being torn between my love for God and my love for my family and friends.

I could not understand why the Lord would expect or ask me not to do something that my family was encouraging me to do. For example, I couldn't grasp why the Lord refused to give me His go-ahead to start a new relationship, even when my family and friends were encouraging me to do so. And the battle, waged in my mind, between following the Ways of the Lord and listening to my family and friends had such a draining effect on me that most of the time I could not even think straight.

I spent years going to my family and friends for their help and advice, and the advice that they would offer me was very pleasing to my flesh but after I had taken some of their advice and suggestions onboard I would still be left dealing with my pain and heartbreak all over again. I even got to a stage where I resented the Lord so much because He would not change His rules for me. (At the time they seemed so impossible.) So like before, in the case of searching in the place called sex, the Lord allowed me to search out this area for myself until I eventually came to the realisation that this place was not going to rid me of my pain.

If this is an area that you are searching through, I would like to suggest that you surrender it to the Lord and allow Him to help you obtain victory over your problems. James Chapter 4 verses 7 and 8 say it like this: *"Submit yourselves therefore to God. Resist the devil, and he will flee from you. Draw nigh to God, and he will draw nigh to you . . ."*

Family and friends are very important to us but they will not have the ability to fully help you during the healing and restoring process. There are just some things that only the Lord can help us with and I guess He has made it this way so that we will always have to go to Him for help and put Him first!

I searched in a place called excitement!

Now let me talk about one of my most favourite places I searched through for my relief — the place called excitement! I do not know anyone who does not like going to this place. It is a great place to be at because of the delightful endless opportunities and feelings that it is able to present us with. I love excitement: the excitement of getting dressed up to go out, the excitement of meeting someone well known, the excitement of achieving a goal, the excitement of receiving a gift, the excitement of being in God's presence, and generally, I just like the excitement of being excited. So when I was going through my heartbreak and could not face up to some of the facts, I naturally decided to dive into this alternative.

In my belief that excitement was the answer to some of my problems, I began to throw myself into the things that I knew would give me excitement. I visited friends, took my son to the park, watched movies, played music, travelled, bought a new car, bought new clothes, did my hair and attended family parties and gatherings. You name it I did it, all in the hope that my excitement would eliminate my pain. And the truth was that being excited usually did blot out my pain, but at the same time, I could not help but notice that this kind of excitement was always short-lived. When the feelings of excitement ended I would still be left with the same old feelings of pain and heartbreak.

Excitement is something that is short-lived and only for a particular moment in time, and it is never expected to last forever. As much as I would have wanted it to last forever I knew this was just not possible and it did not matter how much I tried to kid myself, somehow the truth would always come back and bite me.

We should always thank the Lord for the emotion of excitement, as it is without a doubt helpful to us, but it should not serve as a substitute for the hope that we have in the Lord. I experienced so many exciting times during this dark period of my life, but they did not help me mend my broken heart. They helped me to gloss over the cracks for a little while and even to forget my troubles for a short time, but they did not take away or heal my pain. I was excited but still hurting! Excited but still in pain!

If you are looking for your healing in this place, you will not find it! You can even go on for years believing that one day you will, but the truth is that the healing you need does not exist in this place. The Lord is the only person that can give us the food and drink that we need for our souls (*John 6:35*), and I would like to encourage you to put a stop to your search in this place and to start searching for the Lord. I guarantee you that you will find the healing and restoration that your soul is so desperately longing for.

I explored the place called new relationships!

You may have noticed I have used the word "explored" instead of "searched" in this sub-heading. This is due to the fact that I did not actually search in this place, but I did contemplate the idea of starting a new relationship. I want to address this place because I know that it is a place many of us have found ourselves at. I have studied many individuals as they go through a breakdown of a relationship and one thing that is a common factor in a lot of these cases is that the individuals involved often feel the need to rush into another relationship. This is usually done with the pretence that rushing into a new relationship will help you to get over the other one much quicker and easier.

Well, I experienced this desire and can identify with and relate to some of the reasons why many of us choose to take this step. And I would have searched through this place too if it had not been for the guidance of the Holy Spirit on this matter. I went through regular periods where I begged and pleaded with the Lord to give me His permission to go ahead and start a new relationship, and the only thing that really prevented me from going down this road was that my heartbreak had been so painful that it somehow acted as a deterrent that helped prevent me from crossing this line.

On the few occasions when I have shared this information with someone else, I have usually likened my experience to that of placing my hand in a very hot fire and burning myself, and the fear and pain that I experienced as a result of doing this has mentally prevented me from ever placing my hand back in the same fire again. This comparison would come to mind every time I had those strong urges to start another relationship. Part of me was terrified at the prospect of starting another relationship because of the pain the first one caused me. But on the other hand, part of me longed to be wanted and loved by a man again.

At the time of feeling like this I knew that the Lord loved me but I still could not deny the fact that I desperately wanted to be loved by another human being. Having the love of the Lord was great and He was helping me through my pain so much, but my flesh still longed for the presence of a "real" man in my life. So I kept going to the Holy Spirit and saying, "Am I ready yet?" and, "Please Lord, I really need someone to help me to get over my pain." But each time I would go to Him on the matter His replies would be, "You are not ready yet," or, "I love you," or, "You will only be kidding yourself if you start a new relationship because your heart will not be there."

Well as you can imagine, these were not the answers that I wanted to hear. And I kicked and screamed like a big baby after hearing them, but deep down I knew He was right. As hard as it seemed, every time I experienced these feelings the Lord would give me the strength to make the sensible decision not to go ahead with my own plans and wait on His guidance.

Just like all the other places I searched, this one was not and is still not the answer to heart-break. I have seen and heard of people that have gone down this road and have ended up a lot worse off than they were to begin with. I have heard of cases where a woman entered another relationship in an attempt to free herself from her pain only to find that things are still the same for her because she is still unable to get over the previous relationship. She usually enters into this new relationship thinking she will be able to use it as a tool to help her get over the man she is really in love with, only to find that she ends up comparing the new man to the other man. *Not a great start to a new relationship, would you agree?*

I am so glad that I had the wisdom and strength not to go ahead with my plans to start a new relationship at that particular time, as I could have possibly put myself through a lot more unnecessary heartache.

I know that feelings of rejection and loneliness can be very painful and they can even drive you to do things that you would not normally do, but rushing into a new relationship is not going to relieve your pain. If you are really serious about getting yourself back together and would like to receive total healing and restoration for your broken heart, you will have to go to the Lord and ask Him to help, deliver and heal you.

Looking to your ex for help

As I was drawing near to the end of rewriting this chapter, I stopped to ask the Holy Spirit if there was any other area that He wished for me to share with you. I asked this question because in my spirit I somehow knew that there was something missing from this chapter. As I sat in my CPD training meeting pondering over other areas that I could possibly share with you, the Holy Spirit dropped these words in my spirit: "Looking to your ex for help."

It may sound silly to some, and at this point someone may even be asking, "Why would you look to the one that has supposedly hurt you for help?" So I guess I will just have to say it again — it is one of those things that you will never really understand until you experience it!

I had grown to love this man so much that even after he had hurt me and betrayed all my trust in him, I still believed that he held the keys to my help and healing. I would share the depths of my heart and soul with him with the hope that one day he would have mercy on me and put me out of my misery. I thought that if I shared my pain with him, he would feel badly about what he was putting me through and possibly change his mind and come back to me. My ex-partner was like my God and I really believed that if I kept asking him for help then one day he would eventually relent and stop my pain – but of course that day never came! (Hold on a minute. I sense in my spirit that I need to make something clear to you all before I go on.)

My intentions for writing this book are not and have never been to make this person out to be some kind of heartless rat because he is not. I do realise that the whole thing may have been as stressful for him as it was for me, but like I have said before, I can only share with you what I went through because I lived it.

When he moved on to a new relationship that should have been my cue to move on also, but for some reason I could not find the sense or strength to do it. And the fact that we had finished because we both wanted different things out of a relationship did not change the fact that I still loved him dearly. (Believe me, breaking up because you *have to* and breaking up because you *want to* are two different things!)

I waited months and years for him to help me. I even denied the help of the Holy Spirit because I wanted my help and deliverance to come from this person, but in as much as I still held on to his very word, all I seemed to do was make the separation process much harder. Holding on to him and expecting him to help me out of my pain only gave me mixed messages. I would read things that were not really there into his words and actions and would find myself constantly picking up the broken pieces of my heart as a result.

I have a lot of first-hand experience and knowledge of the problems this can generate, and looking to your ex to help you with your pain in such circumstances will never work. I chose to seek my ex because at the time I believed that I would feel safe and secure with the known, but the reality of it is that it is a false sense of security. Trust me, you would be better off putting your trust and hope in the Lord!

Seriously, how can the person that you are trying to get over really help you? (It took me years to answer this question wisely. I hope that this will not be the case with you.)

All unnecessary searches must come to an end!

I hope that sharing my search has blessed you, answered some of your questions and ministered to your individuals needs, but like all good things it has to come to end. I have been honest with you and shared with you the main places I searched for help, healing and answers for my pain. I have advised and reasoned with you in the best way I know, but the next steps in this process are going to be up to you.

You will have to decide whether or not you are going to continue searching in the wrong places for your deliverance, whether or not you will allow the Holy Spirit to safely guide you through to the end, and whether or not you will kill your flesh and start walking in the fruit of the Spirit *(see Galatians 5:16-26)*.

What happens next will be up to you! But I pray that the Lord will strengthen you and help you make the right decisions *(see Proverbs 8:10-11)*. From this point on you may still have to experience some very hard times and really tough experiences, especially when you decide to do it God's Way, but one thing is for certain and that is this: *"You can do all things through Christ Jesus who strengthens you"* (Philippians 4:1).

Chapter Six

Get a grip on your mind!

*"For though we walk in the flesh, we do not war after the flesh: (For the weapons of our warfare are not carnal, but mighty through God to the pulling down of strong holds;) Casting down imaginations, and every high thing that exalteth itself against the knowledge of God, **and bringing into captivity every thought to the obedience of Christ;**"*

2 Corinthians 10:3-5 (KJV)

My desire to discuss this issue has been largely influenced by my own personal struggle in this area. The battle of the mind was without a doubt one of the hardest struggles I had to overcome. I feel a great burden to address this subject matter because I sense in my spirit there might be many of you also struggling in this area. My main purpose for writing this next chapter, titled "Get a grip on your mind," is to help you breakthrough and overcome one of the biggest battles of all — controlling your mind!

All the bodily organs God has blessed us with are equally important to us, but when I think about the mind I cannot help wonder how difficult my life would be if I did not have a sound one. The mind is very important and it is extremely necessary for us to keep our minds in good working order, as this will enable us to effectively carry out our daily tasks and divine purpose. As a believer in Christ, it is essential to our well-being that we continue to follow the teachings of God's Word by *"not copying the behaviour and customs of this world, but by letting God transform us into a new person by changing the way we think"* (Romans 12:2, NLT).

Human beings are made up of three main sub-parts: the body (flesh), the spirit, and the soul. Let me put it like this: we are spirit beings who live in a body and we have a soul. The mind is part of our soul and it includes our thoughts, feelings, consciousness, intellect, and will. It is also the place where all the words that we say and actions that we carry out are first thought up, and if we are not careful in regards to some of the things that we choose to meditate on, the mind will govern all that we do and say, both good and bad!

The Word of God is able to reach and touch people at a collective and personal level, and God often allows His children to receive different revelations from the same piece of Scripture at various times. Take Proverbs 23:7 for example: "For as he thinks in His heart, so is he." When I first heard this Scripture verse many years ago, the revelation that I got from it was that we have to be very careful with regards to the thoughts we allow to entertain our minds and the condition of our hearts because these things will determine the person that we are or may become.

Although I spent a lot of time skimming through the Word of God, and I was familiar with some of the Scriptures concerning the subject of controlling the mind, it was not until the Holy Spirit led me to Joyce Meyer's book *Battlefield of the Mind, Winning the Battle in your Mind* that I actually realised that my mind and thinking were messed up and contrary to the Word of God.

Before reading Joyce Meyer's book, it had not occurred to me in the slightest that a war was being waged against my mind. I was completely blinded to this truth and I did not realise that I was literally living in a spiritual battlefield. I was so innocent. I naively thought that my mental struggle was part of a normal process that everyone went through and that I would just have to somehow learn to cope with it.

When I think back on this whole affair, I really do thank the Lord for the grace and mercies He bestowed on me during my time of ignorance, and I truly appreciate the fact that He did not abandon me but instead chose to help, warn, prepare, and equip me for the battle that I was about to face *(see Psalm 18:39)*.

It was only when I took the time to read Joyce Meyer's book that my spiritual eyes were opened and I was able to properly recognise the struggle within my mind. After reading this book, I finally realised that my only hope of ever defeating the devil was to use the Word of God — my weapon — and the Holy Spirit — my helper. It is a very powerful book and I credit much of my breakthrough to the knowledge and understanding that I received from reading it. (If you are struggling with the subject of controlling your mind, I would strongly recommend that you obtain and read this book — it will really help and bless you!)

On my journey from heartbreak to complete freedom, I had to fight the battle of gaining back control of my mind by learning to control the thoughts and images that I allowed to enter it. I had to fight the battle by renewing my mind with the Word of God. I had to fight the devil in a game at which he's an expert and I was a novice. I had to trust the Lord at a time when I really did not want to, and there were also times when I had to go against my own way of doing things and choose to believe the Lord, even when I did not understand why I was making this choice. To say that overcoming the battle in my mind was challenging would be an understatement. However, when I eventually decided to fight back and get a grip on my mind, the Lord was right there to give me a complete victory. As we move on through this chapter, I intend to share how I personally conquered this obstacle of getting a grip on my mind.

We will look at the three main issues that I had to experience in my desperate fight to gain back control of my mind. In the first part, I will explain the state of my mind before I realised that an actual battle was being waged against it — my messed up mind!; in the following part, I will discuss the battle for control over my mind that I experienced after I realised that I myself would have to fight to gain this control back, and in the final part, I will discuss the victory that I eventually got over the devil after I decided to trust and obey the Lord.

My messed-up mind!

Before I began to read the Word of God, I used to think that my mind and thoughts were fine. I simply believed that my way of thinking was normal and I assumed that all the thoughts and ideas that entered my mind were constructive and essential to the kind of person that I was. I even believed this about the negative thoughts I had. My justification for these kinds of thoughts was that they are only my response to the insensitive words or actions of other people who have wronged me. I thought I was well within my rights to react in any way that I wanted. I used to believe that I was right the majority of the time and other people would have to adapt to my way of thinking if they were ever going to relate to me. (I was a bit arrogant in this sense, and did not think anything of it!)

For as long as I can remember, I have always been strong-willed. I loved this quality about me because it allowed me to achieve many things and get a lot of things done. I would simply meditate on what I wanted to gain and then I would not give up my pursuit until I had it. I was and still am very persistent and wilful.

Now, apart from the fact that my thinking used to be quite messed up during this time and my motives were often way off the mark, I don't apologise for the fact that I was, and still am, quite a wilful person. Personally, I don't think there is anything wrong with someone having a wilful mind. The only real problem that I have with anyone having this kind of quality or approach is when the motives and thinking behind their tenacity is wrong. Other than that, I thank the Lord that I have been blessed with this quality and if you have it too, and your motives are pure, you should not be ashamed of it either. The problem is not really with us having a wilful mind, the problem is with who and what we allow to access and dominate our minds.

I sense in my spirit that some of you may be a little surprised or confused by my last comment, so I included this portion of Scripture to help clear some things up: In the New Living Translation of the Bible, in Romans 8:5-8, it tells us that, *"Those that are dominated by the sinful nature think about sinful things, but those who are controlled by the Holy Spirit think about things that please the Spirit. So letting your sinful nature control your mind leads to death. But letting the Spirit control your mind leads to life and peace. For the sinful nature is always hostile to God. It never did obey God's laws, and it never will. That's why those who are still under the control of their sinful nature can never please God."* God gave us each a mind and will to think and do things for ourselves; He doesn't want us to be robots! It was never His intention for us not to use these attributes for what they were intended — and we can undeniably use them for whatever we choose.

Before I aligned myself with the Word of God and started to think more about the things that were pleasing to Him, I did not realise that I was allowing my sinful nature to dominate my thinking. As far as I was concerned my thinking was fine — a bit crazy at times, but fine!

I believe that there are three beings constantly competing for the attention of our minds: the Spirit of God, yourself, and the devil. And if you are not careful or aware of this, it can trigger a battle in your mind for obvious reasons. As a believer in Jesus Christ it is essential for us to take heed and obey the voice and guidance of the Holy Spirit so that He can teach us how we can be successful in having power and control over our minds and the devil.

As a baby Christian, I was not fully aware of this, so I gave my consent for all three sources to have their say in my mind. My lack of knowledge and understanding regarding this left me open to all the arrows that the devil sent my way, and I ignorantly took all those shots like a stupid soldier. If anyone had told me beforehand the depths of pain and distress that I would have to endure as a direct result of my ignorance and unwillingness to cooperate with the Holy Spirit, I would never have believed them. I just did not see it coming, and I certainly could not have fully comprehended the brutality of the thoughts and feelings that were waged against my mind by the devil, all with the sole intention of destroying me!

From the moment I found out my ex-partner had started a new

relationship, I slowly began to lose control of my mind. I had not expected this to happen so soon after we had broken up, so it totally took me by surprise and knocked me right off my feet. And instantaneously, my mind began to race at a faster rate than I had ever experienced before.

Like I have mentioned before in a previous chapter, the first battle in my mind that I had to deal with was disbelief and denial. I could not believe that he had chosen to do something so hurtful to me, knowing full-well that there could still be a possibility of us getting back together. My mind went into overdrive and began to think about things from how much I hated him to how much I loved him, as well as speculating why he had chosen to do this to me and the part I had played in initiating the split. I even wondered if his new girl was prettier than me, if he really liked her better than me, and so forth.

To go through and write down all the thoughts and feelings that I had would take up so much time, so I will sum it up in these words: every thought or feeling that you can imagine as a result of these circumstances, I had. And you can be rest assured that the devil made it his duty to bring to my attention the ones that I did not have of my own accord. Not only did I have thoughts and scenarios about my present situation, but they soon escalated to actual video images playing in my mind. If they were helpful video images, I probably would not have minded them so much, but they were not helpful to me at all. The video images were usually of my ex-partner in loving scenarios with his new partner and things like that, and they would play over and over again in my mind, tormenting me. They absolutely wounded me and added to my existing distress!

The negative thoughts and feelings went on for what seemed like years and I grew to accept them. I did not believe that I could ever escape them, so the only other option I thought I had was to accept them, and this is what I ignorantly did. I even got to a point where I was spending around ninety percent of my time thinking about this problem. It was enormous! It became the first thing on my mind every morning as I woke up, it was something that I would think about frequently throughout the day, and it was the last thing I would think about as I was about to fall asleep. The thoughts would come and I would try my best to fend them off, only to be left with a new set of upsetting thoughts and feelings to contend with all over again.

Before I eventually made up my mind to obey the Lord's advice and fight back, it would be a fair assessment to say that my mind was a mess and that I had given the devil most of the control over it. I say most of it and not all because the fact that I still had the strength and ability to eventually obey and follow the Holy Spirit's directions meant that I had to have some form of control of my mind.

I don't remember the reason or circumstances related to the moment when I first purchased Joyce Meyer's book, but it was the best thing I could have done at that particular time. Apart from the fact that Meyer makes a lot of reference to Biblical Scriptures concerning the renewal and control of our minds, and I had been familiar with some of them, the fact that she had struggled with this area and had overcome this same battle was extremely encouraging to me. The contents of this book helped to shed new light on my own situation and the result of reading it was like a blindfold being removed from my eyes.

Meyer's book really helped me, and it was only after reading it that I found the strength to make it my sincere purpose in my heart to work together with the Holy Spirit to fight the devil and take back full control of my mind. I had had enough and I wasn't going to allow my thoughts and feelings to defeat me anymore. I chose to use my weapon — the Word of God!

This all sounds great, right? And you are probably thinking to yourselves, "Great, a breakthrough!" Well, the truth is that things got worse. For the mere fact that I had made the decision to rise up and fight back, the devil also made a decision to step up his game against me and the thoughts and images that he placed in my mind from that moment on became more intense than ever before. The battle was really on!

When a negative thought or image came to my mind, I would confess relevant Scriptures from the Word of God and meditate on them until I actually believed it. But if I am honest, this approach only worked for me sometimes; and there were other times when it did not. There were many times when I could not handle the pressure and I would just crumble and cry out in pain at the barrage of thoughts that I experienced. At times I would feel really strong, but at other times, I would just buckle under the constant torment.

Joyce Meyer's book lists quite a lot of relevant Scriptures, which I took and started to use as my weapon. One of the main Scriptures that captured my heart, and still stands out to me now, is Proverbs 3:5-6: *"Trust in the Lord with all thine heart: and lean not unto thine understanding. In all thy ways acknowledge him, and he shall direct thy paths"* (KJV). I confessed and meditated on these verses nearly every opportunity I had. I would even confess this Bible Scripture when I was not experiencing an attack on my mind. I loved it and still do.

My association with this book definitely helped to give me the wisdom, strength, and courage I needed to prepare for my first battle with the devil and it was at this point that I retaliated and began my fight for my mind!

My mind struggle!

On the back cover of Joyce Meyer's book there is a heading which reads, "There's a War Going On And Your Mind Is The Battlefield." This declaration really does sum up in a nutshell the battle that I had been enlisted into. The devil had occupied and controlled my mind for so long because of this situation that he probably believed he had the right to be there and as you would expect, he was not about to leave without a fight. Whenever I would start to believe that my thoughts could not get any more distressing than they already were, I was mistaken!

After my spiritual eyes were opened to this revelation, my thoughts got much worse and more frequent. I am going to be totally honest with you, and tell you that to begin with it seemed like I had taken on more than I could chew in this battle. The devil must have said to himself, "If she is going to be brave enough to take me on, I am going to use all the power that I possibly can to make sure that she does not succeed." When I say that the devil tried every trick in the book, I mean exactly that — every trick in the book! He used the "fire it all at me at once" approach, which would often leave me in fits of tears and distress, the "lay low and stay quiet until the next attack" approach, which would leave me believing that everything was alright for a short while. He used the "get others to make comments and suggestions to me" approach, which would leave me in a state of confusion, and he also used the "if you compromise God's law" approach, which would leave me questioning the Lord's ability to actually bring me through the battle. He basically used every weapon that he had to get me to change my mind and back down.

Looking back on the period when I decided to follow the Holy Spirit's lead to turn around my situation and stand up to the devil, I think I was a bit naïve. I was naïve in thinking that it would be a simple battle and I really believed that the Lord would just click His fingers and the devil would back down, just like that. It never occurred to me that the Lord would use this opportunity to test and turn me into the warrior that He wanted me to be.

I thought that by confessing and meditating on the relevant Scriptures for short periods of time, this would give me the quick victory I so desperately needed. So I would read my Bible when the attacks would come, but when everything seemed fine, I would not return to it for weeks. I did not realise that I was supposed to always be ready and prepared for war, or that the Word of God was the only weapon that had the power to put the devil in his place. I really underestimated the devil and as a result of this, I continued to suffer and lose the mind battle. One minute I would be in the lead and the next minute the devil would regain his ground, but unlike me, the devil was experienced!

The battle was not going the way I believed it should have been going, so I used to regularly go to the Holy Spirit in my state of confusion and ask Him, "Why are you not helping me when you said that you would?"

"Why are you not helping me to defeat the devil?" It never occurred to me before that the disobedience of my sexual sin and the struggle for my mind could be connected in any way. And even when the devil would remind and taunt me about my present lack of commitment to the Lord in this area, I was still unable to make this connection.

The Holy Spirit would tell me over and over again that I had to ask Him to help me cut the unhealthy soul tie and stop having sex with my ex, but I would not take any notice and continued to carry on living my double life. I would describe my struggle at this time as: trying to fight a battle on both sides of the camp. On one hand, I was in the Lord's army, mainly because I desperately needed some help in overcoming my pain, and on the other hand I was ignorantly helping the devil to destroy me. It was a very confusing battle!

Despite all the circumstances and my own ignorance, the Lord stayed with me through it all. He never left my side. The Lord knew that if I continued to press on and seek Him, I would eventually learn from my mistakes and make wiser choices and decisions. And this is exactly what happened — I continued to battle on and became a more experienced solider.

My battle was no different from the actual military ones that you usually see on the news or in films — it was extremely serious! I went through periods of feeling like I had defeated the devil to moments of total weakness. I experienced low and high periods. There were times when I felt so weak that the thought of having to fight on would make me feel physically sick, and I even went through periods where I truly believed that the Lord had forsaken me. My battle was so long that at times I would often wonder to myself: *Is it ever going to end?* And it wasn't until I got to the place in my fight where it became all or nothing that things started to change!

My Victory!

In 2 Corinthians 10:5, the Apostle Paul talks about using spiritual weapons God has given us in our battle for gaining control over the unproductive thoughts that constantly bombard our minds. Let me share this Scripture with you again so you can see exactly what it says. Let's read from verse 3 to 5: *". . . for though we walk in the flesh, we do not war after the flesh: (for the weapons of our warfare are not carnal, but mighty through God to the pulling down of strong holds;) Casting down imaginations, and every high thing that exalteth itself against the knowledge of God, and bringing into captivity every thought to the obedience of Christ."(KJV)*

It took me ages to get the revelation behind this Scripture and to come to terms with what it actually meant concerning my own battle with my mind. I read it over and over again at various times prior to this moment, but I still couldn't understand or believe it. (How many of you know that it can be possible to read something over and over again without being able to understand or believe in what you have just read?)

I often wonder to myself how strange it is that most believers find it easy to believe and apply some Scriptures over others, but will often find it hard to believe and apply *all* of the Scriptures in the Bible. For example, let's take Joshua Chapter 1 verses 7-8, which says, *"Be strong and courageous. Be careful to obey all the instructions Moses gave you. Do not deviate from them, turning either to the right or to the left. Then you will be successful in everything you do. Study this book of Instruction continually. Meditate on it day and night so you will be sure to obey everything written in it.* Now, how many of us have read or have heard these words before, but even after receiving this word have still continued to disobey the Lord or have not meditated on the Bible for days and weeks? Probably all of us right!

The point that I am trying to make is that many of us claim to believe, but do we really believe? If we truly believe that the Word of God is a book of instructions that will help us to be successful, prosperous and live a Godly fulfilling life, then what really is the problem? I would say the problem is our lack of belief, trust and faith in God's full capability! It's not that we don't always want to believe — sometimes it's just hard to believe!

It was my unbelief in the Lord's ability to actually bring me through that kept me on the battlefield for so long. I was confessing the right Scriptures and saying the right things, but did I really believe in my heart of hearts that the Lord would give me total victory? The answer is no. I did not really believe, and it was only when I acknowledged that this was actually the case that the Holy Spirit was able to help me overcome this and things started to change.

My turning point occurred when I made up my mind to meditate on and trust the words of the apostle Paul. It was my turning point from constantly battling to winning the victory over my mind. The more I studied this Scripture the more I began to realise that most of the thoughts I had spent so much of my time meditating on were not even an actual reality. Most of the issues that I used to spend all my time pondering over for days and months were not even happening in the physical sense; they were just a figment of my wild imagination. You see, reality to a believer in Jesus Christ can be defined as anything written in the Word of God and the things that first happen in the spiritual realm. Whereas to a non-believer and believers that don't really believe, reality is what they can see.

The Word of God is the only reality that I should have been meditating on, believing and confessing during that period. *"Casting down imaginations, and every high thing that exalteth itself against the knowledge of God, and bringing into captivity every thought to the obedience of Christ,"* is what I should have been doing from the first day that I read those Scriptures, but instead of believing the Word of God, I continued to let those imaginations exalt themselves above the knowledge of the all knowing God.

The day I began to really trust in these verses was the day I began to gain victory over my mind and I was able to confidently fight back against the devil. Little by little I began to cast down every negative thought that came to my mind, right from the onset, and instead of giving into them I began to meditate on the Word of God and my vision to reach my God-given destiny. The Lord gave me the victory in this battle, and walking in this victory over the devil was such a liberating feeling. The state of my mind went from being totally confused and overloaded with rubbish to being peaceful and more focused. I was able to freely think about those things that I was supposed to be meditating on, such as the Word of God, and the fact that I was now able to do this meant that the Holy Spirit could now help me build up my spirit and teach me how to become victorious in other areas of my life.

God is not a respecter of persons (*Acts 10:34*) and everything that I have told you concerning what He has done for me in my life is what He desires to do for you. He wants you to have a sound mind (*see 2 Timothy 1:7*) so that you can live a successful and abundant life here on earth. If you are struggling to get a grip on your mind I would strongly recommend that you take my advice and ask the Holy Spirit to show you how you can be victorious in your own circumstances.

I want you to remember that the Holy Spirit is your comforter and helper (*see John 14:16*) and that He is waiting patiently for your invitation to assist you in your situation. So I encourage you to allow Him to help you fight and win the battle within your mind!

Let us pray!

Father, I thank you that even now as we begin to pray, You are healing, restoring and renewing our minds. It is not Your will that we should be struggling in this area, and for this reason, let us declare, "I have a sound mind (2 Timothy 1:7), the mind of Christ, and through Him I can do all things! In the name of Jesus, I take full control over every negative thought, idea, and way of thinking that is contrary to the Word and mind of Christ — and I pull it down (2 Corinthians 10:5). No weapon formed against my mind shall prosper (Isaiah 54:17), and with the empowerment of the Holy Spirit, I will surely press on to reach my divine destination!"

Amen.

Chapter Seven

The Lord's deliverance and healing power!

"I will bless the Lord at all times: his praise shall continually be in my mouth. My soul shall make her boasts in the Lord: the humble shall hear thereof, and be glad. O magnify the Lord with me, and let us exalt his name together. I sought the Lord, and he heard me, and delivered me from all my fears . . . The eyes of the Lord are upon the righteous, and his ears are open unto their cry . . . The righteous cry, and the Lord heareth, and delivereth them out of all their troubles. The Lord is nigh unto them that are of a broken heart; and saveth such as be of a contrite spirit. Many are the afflictions of the righteous: but the Lord delivereth him out of them all."

Psalms 34:1-4, 15, 17-19, KJV

As I read through Psalms 34, I cannot help but notice the sweeping sensation of great peace and joy that has come over my soul. I am so excited to be reading these reassuring words at this moment in time. I cannot remember the first time I heard it, or even when I first read this Psalm, but what I do know is that my understanding of it today has been totally enlightened. I remember reading it years ago and thinking to myself, *I wonder if such words could possibly become true in my own situation?* And now, as I read through it all these years later, I can without a doubt declare to the world that these words are absolutely true for me — they have become a reality in my life!

As I contemplated how I would begin this seventh chapter, the Holy Spirit woke me in the early hours of the morning to share this Psalm with me. He told me to begin this chapter with this Psalm, and in particular verses 17-19. I went back to sleep soon after, but as soon as I woke up the following morning I grabbed my Bible and began to read it. *What a revelation*! I thought to myself.

My purpose for including this chapter is to first testify to the Lord's goodness and mercies towards me, and secondly to reassure you that if you cry out to the Lord and ask Him for help, He will hear your cries and rescue you too. So the fact that the Lord has placed this Psalm on my heart at this particular moment is so fitting.

In the lead-up to actually writing this chapter, I came to a crossroad. I was a little confused about how I would set it out and I did not know which direction to take, so I simply asked the Holy Spirit to guide me. Although I was a little unsure, I did not let this setback discourage me in any way because I was certain that the Holy Spirit would come through for me in the end. I made a conscious decision to wake up in the morning like I usually did to start writing and wait on the Lord. So I got up in the morning and did just that.

As I sat on my bed meditating on the words of the song "I don't mind waiting" by Juanita Bynum, the Holy Spirit began to direct my paths and the instructions that I desperately needed began to flow — it was as simple as that!

The Holy Spirit instructed me to share four main areas with you: my struggles, the point where I gave up my own fight and surrendered all, the moment I experienced God's breakthrough and healing power, and the gradual process the Lord had to take me through to reach the place where I could freely testify of His faithfulness and all that He had done for me.

As you read this chapter, I want you to read it with an expectant heart. I want you to believe that the Lord can do the same for you. What I do not want is for you to read through this chapter and say to yourselves, "Wow, did the Lord really do that for Sasha?" But instead, I want you to read though my account and say, "Lord, I will wait on You for my deliverance and healing because You said in Your Word that You would hear my cries for help and rescue me from my broken heart and crushed spirit!"

Mark 11:23-24 says, *"For verily I say unto you, That whosoever shall say unto this mountain, Be thou removed, and be thou cast into the sea: and shall not doubt in his heart, but shall believe that those things which he saith shall come to pass; he shall have whatsoever he saith. Therefore I say unto you, What things so ever ye desire, when ye pray, believe that ye receive them, and ye shall have them"* (KJV). If your desire is for the Lord to heal you of your pain and set you free, you will have to trust in the Lord Jesus Christ with all your heart, believe and confess God's Word, and follow the guidance of the Holy Spirit. Trust me, I did it and it works!

The struggle!

Throughout this book, I have openly shared and discussed with you in great detail a lot of the struggles that I experienced on my journey with the Lord from heartbreak to restoration. I have talked about the struggles that I encountered in learning to take God at His Word, my struggle with letting go of worthless things, and my struggle to get a grip on my mind and situation. Although I have experienced all these different struggles and talk about them separately, there was one common factor that linked them all together; they were all struggles with my flesh! *(See Galatians 5:19-21)*

I struggled with my flesh for years. I blamed myself, others, and even the Lord for the position I found myself in. I spent so much time trying to shift the blame away from myself that never once did it occur to me that I could be the problem. My lack of knowledge concerning all of this made me ignorant to this fact! *(See Hosea 4:6)*

The apostle Paul lists all the works of the flesh in Galatians 5:19-21. *(Please read through these Scriptures)*. Would you agree with me that they do exist in your Bible? (If you haven't already done so, why don't you go and take a look for yourself right now; they are written as clear as can be.)

Well the truth is I have known of their existence for as long as I can remember. And I even read these Scriptures when I was going through my distress. But for some reason, maybe defiance, I seemed to bypass the part where the apostle Paul wrote, ". . . those who do such things shall not inherit the kingdom of God." Somehow, I did not think that it applied to me!

As a young Christian I suppose it is more than likely that you would take the parts of Scriptures that are pleasing to your flesh and disregard the bits that you don't really like for one reason or another, but for a more matured Christian I would say that this practice is less acceptable. In my experience many young Christians do this, and I was no exception. I wanted the Lord to help me out of my situation but at the same time, I was not prepared to completely listen to or follow His counsel to get out of my mess.

I knew that Jesus Christ was able to help people in their time of need because I had heard so many testimonies to this fact, but what I did not realise was that when most people share their testimonies concerning the Lord's help and intervention, they usually play down the parts where they also had to kill their flesh, be obedient and give something up in order to receive their breakthrough.

If I am completely honest with you, my real struggles with this issue started when I decided to take up the Lord's offer of help. Like I said before, I had been acquainted with the Lord for a few years prior to the moment that I cried out to Him. Although, during this time, I had not spent as much time as I could have developing my relationship with Him. To be honest with you, I did not know that my flesh would try and prevent me from doing this, so I ignorantly struggled on trying to fight my own battle.

The little knowledge that I had of the Lord during this time was gained from a small number of close Christian friends, occasionally attending church and flicking through my new Spirit Filled Living Bible. Other than that, I did not have any great desire to follow the Lord or His Way. (I would not go as far as to say that the Lord never meant anything to me at this time, He just was not as important to me as many of the other things in my life.)

I decided to ask the Lord for His help soon after I was left devastated by the breakdown of this relationship. I cannot remember the exact reason why I chose to do this, but it was probably as a result of the advice of friends or my realisation that nothing else could help me. It initially started off with me going to the Lord at night when I had finished running to and fro for the day, from friend to friend and thought to thought. Night time was the worst time of all for me, as this was the time when I was left alone with all those images and thoughts to deal with. And as much as I would have loved to have called a friend for a chat to help me through them, I somehow knew that my actions would not really be appreciated in the early hours of the morning. I started to talk to the Holy Spirit about my feelings, inadequacies, hurt and pain. I would talk to Him about almost everything and anything from college, to my son, to my weaknesses, to my pain, to my future, and my desires.

These late night chats with the Holy Spirit were definitely a step in the right direction because they gave me a sense of release from the heaviness I had been experiencing during the day. They also helped me to realise that the Lord does actually listen to the ones that He loves. The Holy Spirit didn't do much talking in the beginning and would just allow me to pour out my heart and soul to Him, but I later began to realise that He also wanted to speak, and I eventually learned to hear and listen to the voice of God for myself.

During this time, I had not been completely obedient to the Lord and I was still struggling heavily with my flesh, but nevertheless, I made a decision to carry on and develop my relationship with the Lord despite this struggle.

It was simple! I finally got to the stage where I did not care how others perceived me or whether or not they thought I was being a hypocrite for living a double life. I simply decided to take God at His Word and came to Him as I was. (*See Matthew 11:28*)

Directly seeking the Lord and learning to converse with Him proved to be a primary turning point. And with the help of the Holy Spirit, I began to follow some of His instructions. I started to build up my self-esteem and confidence with the Word of God, I was gaining more and more control over my mind and actions and I was also learning how to use my spiritual authority in certain areas in my life. So then, if this was the case, why was I still feeling the painful effects of my broken heart?

The answer to this question is quite simple and deep down, I knew full-well why I was still struggling with my issue — *it was because I was still having sex with my ex-partner!*

The Holy Spirit had told me so many times throughout my situation that I should stop having sex with my ex-partner if I really wanted to be free and move on, but for some reason, unknown to me at the time, I could not do it. I even got to the stage where I refused to speak with the Holy Spirit about this subject. I told Him, "Lord, you don't understand the love and connection that this man and I have, so just leave this part of my life to me. I will deal with it." I refused point-blank to listen to the Holy Spirit's counsel on this matter and even when He used other people to share this wisdom with me, I still refused to listen to Him.

For me, I would say that by far the biggest struggle I contended with in this entire situation was the struggle to give up this man. I say this because it was the only struggle that I did not seem to be gaining victory over. I had willingly given over the rest of my struggles to the Lord and had experienced victory in those areas, but I just couldn't seem to hand this one over! The devil had a complete stronghold over me in this area and the fact that I would not give the Holy Spirit my permission to free me from it prevented me from being released.

I struggled tremendously with the issue of sexual sin, and even a few years after my heartbreak had occurred and the Lord was building me up and teaching me about the spiritual authority that I possessed as a believer, I still struggled with this sin. In all my worldly thinking about my situation, I had somehow convinced myself that if I continued to have sex with this man I could still have some part in his life. Don't ask me how I came to this conclusion because I wouldn't be able to explain it now, but at the time, it really did seem like a reasonable line of thinking.

From the moment I became broken-hearted to the point where I had to make up my mind whether or not I was going to surrender it all to the Lord, all my struggles had narrowed down to this one decision — was I going to stick with the one who had caused me and was still causing me so much pain or was I going to go with the One who had heard my cries for help, showed me pure love and wanted to heal and restore my broken heart and soul?

I surrender all!

My relationship with my ex-boyfriend officially ended in October 1998 and I did not stop having sex with him until November 2002. He started his other relationship in early 1999, so it does not take a genius to do the math and come to the conclusion that for about three whole years, I was having sex with a person who I knew was also having sex with someone else. Some people may say that this could never happen to them or that they would never do something like this, but the truth is that before this happened to me I used to say this too. The one thing that I have learned in all of this is to never say never!

Choosing to have sex with him while he was seeing someone else is not a decision that I am particularly proud of, and if I could turn back time I would definitely do things differently. But what's done is done and there is no point in beating myself up over the past because it would not change the fact that I made a bad choice. At times like this, I really do thank the Lord for reassuring words such as these: *"There is therefore now no condemnation to them which are in Christ Jesus, who walk not after the flesh, but after the Spirit. For the law of the Spirit of life in Christ Jesus hath made me free from the law of sin and death"* (Romans 8:1-2, KJV).

In the beginning, I didn't really care about what I was doing or who I was hurting, and I definitely did not think that my own actions would end up hurting me. I was just following the lead of my flesh, like I had always done. Even when the Holy Spirit brought my inappropriate behaviour and actions to my attention and made it clear to me that I would have to give this man up, I was still not deterred!

I have always been a persistent person and I can remember from a young age wearing my mother down with my persistent nagging. So naturally, when I could see that the Lord was not giving in to me, I decided that I would use this approach and wear Him down to the point where He would have to grant me my wishes. Out of respect for the Lord, and the fact that I knew I was treading on unfamiliar ground, I decided to go a bit more gently with Him. I didn't harass Him with my hardcore persistent nagging like I had often done with my mother. Instead, I chose the much simpler approach of plain old-fashioned persistence.

As I mentioned before, by this point I had already told the Lord that I would do anything that He wanted me to do, apart from give up this man, and I was not prepared to negotiate my terms and conditions with anyone, including the Lord! I had heard it said many times before that the Word of God never changes, but this was fine by me because according to me, my word never changed either. So I deliberately determined in my mind to carry on doing my thing with this man until the Lord saw the sense in it and changed His mind.

At this stage in my life I believed that I had the best of both worlds. I had the Lord on my side anytime I wanted Him, and I still had a connection with the man that I loved more than anything in this world. The fact that I loved this man so desperately totally blinded any better judgement I may have had to the point where if the Lord had said to me that the sky was blue and this man had said it was yellow, I would have believed him over the Lord. It was as if my ex-boyfriend was my God and my Lord and Saviour Jesus Christ was just my god. I had it so bad that I can even remember the feeling of being physically sick at the thought of having to live without some kind of interaction with this man in my life. *My Lord, I had it really bad!* I can smile about it all now, but there was a moment in time when I really did have it that bad. It did not matter how much I wanted to or how hard I tried, I just could not and did not have the strength I needed to make the sensible decision to stop having sex with this man.

The Lord was so good to me during this period and He still continued to encourage and support me in my state of partial obedience. He obviously knew what was going to come next for me and knew that it would not have been a good idea to leave me completely to my own devises.

Well, the "good times" eventually came to an end and I simply no longer loved this person anymore. I had come to a stage where I also hated him. My feelings of total love for this person were slowly turning into mixed feelings of love and hatred. (When you feel like you are giving your all to someone and they are not returning the favour, this can easily become the case — and it certainly did for me!)

The more I read the Bible and meditated on the Word and things that the Lord said about me, the more it began to dawn on me that I was making a very big mistake. I began to think to myself, "Why and how could I put a man before God?" I started to weigh up all the things the Lord had done and wanted to do for me, with all the things that this man did and did not do for me, and guess what? This man's love did not even compare to the love that I believed the Lord had for me!

Eventually I made the sensible decision to back down and hand this final issue over to the Lord, and as you can imagine, it was not as straightforward as I would have liked it to be. The careless words I had spoken over my own situation in relation to the negative confessions that I had made about not giving up this man had come back to haunt me, and they were holding me hostage! The more I promised the Lord I would not go back and have sex with this man, the more I would have to go back to the Lord in repentance concerning this same old sin.

This practice went on for ages and I cannot remember the number of prayer lines I went down to ask for help in conquering my sexual sin. I read books, listened to messages, and even bought and borrowed tapes on this subject matter, but I still would go back and have sex with this man. By the end of it all, I had enough wisdom on this subject to educate an entire country, but it did not matter because I still could not even apply this wisdom to my own life.

By now I had tried everything I could think of and the whole situation was really starting to get me down. Deep down in my heart, I desperately wanted to please the Lord and refrain from pre-material sex, but my flesh was so weak that I was even starting to believe in my mind that I would never have the strength to do it.

"Do you know what Lord? Maybe we might have to accept that in my case it isn't going to work," I said to the Holy Spirit one day. "Lord, I just can't seem to do what you require of me . . . I just can't do it!" (By this point I was feeling so hopeless. And I could not help but feel I was letting the Lord down by the fact that I kept compromising myself and going back.) "Lord, I can't do it . . . please, will you help me . . . please, will you help to conquer my sin, heal my broken heart and set me free?"

I had finally realised that I could not actually do this thing in my own strength and to me, it was as if the Lord had been waiting patiently for me to acknowledge this weakness so that He could then take over and act on my behalf.

When I made those verbal confessions and surrendered it all to the Lord, I gave the Holy Spirit the permission He had so patiently been waiting for to intervene in my situation. It had taken me a long while but I had finally come to a place where all the kicking, screaming, pushing, trying, and trusting in myself ceased. I was now ready to put my full trust in the Lord and let Him take over. (Yes, I had finally come to the realisation that the Lord had been right all along and I was going to have to give this man up, if not for the Lord, then for my own sanity.)

Breakthrough!

Throughout all my struggles the Lord has always been totally honest with me and has not withheld any of His wisdom from me. The Lord had shown me countless times, through Biblical teachings and the Holy Spirit that it was not His will for me to have sex with someone I was not married to. And at this point, I would like to tell you that it had never occurred to me that this could be part of the problem preventing my breakthrough, but I would be lying — it had occurred to me!

I had tried it my way for so long and the matter only got worse, so the fact that I had now made the decision to hand this burden over to the Lord felt like a big weight lifted from my shoulders.

I began to train my mind to focus more on the things of God as opposed to focusing on my current problems. I read the Word of God more than I had ever done before, and not only did I read it, I also started to study and meditate on it. I found Scriptures that related to the emotions and struggles I was experiencing and began to confess them aloud, and very soon, little by little, I became stronger.

It was at this point that I could really see that the Holy Spirit was at work in me and He was beginning to break and remove certain fleshly mindsets and thought patterns that I had. The Lord's healing and deliverance process had definitely begun in me!

In January 2003, a woman of God came to visit me at my home. She had been in the country on vacation and was brought to my home by my son's dad to pray with my son. While at my home she also requested to pray with me. After the prayers had ended she counselled us for a little while and then left. But before leaving, she told me that I should carry out a two-week fast in order to find out what the Lord had in store for me.

When she left I was determined to fast because I really wanted to hear from the Lord. But to cut a long story short, for some reason or another I did not get around to doing the fast and I eventually forgot about it, until one day almost three months later, while speaking to a friend, it came up in conversation.

As I shared what happened in the meeting at my home with the woman of God, my friend seemed quite shocked at the fact that I had not carried out the fast. "It does not matter how long ago this instruction was given to you Sasha," she said. "You still have to do it!" My friend's reaction to this alarmed me and I really did want to hear from the Lord, so I took heed and determined in my heart to carry out the fast. I finished the conversation with my friend and immediately apologised to the Lord for not being obedient in this instance. I then made a promise to the Lord that I would carry out the two-week fast during my Easter break from university.

About two weeks after I had made this commitment, I embarked on one of the longest fasts I have ever experienced. I spent the next two weeks immersed in the presence of the Lord. I read my Bible, read my old journal notes, praised and worshiped the Lord, and spoke and listened to the Holy Spirit. I had such a great time in the presence of the Lord during this time, and like the woman of God had predicted the Lord answered many of the questions I had been seeking answers for. This was undeniably a time of great breakthrough for me!

The two-week fast just happened to be coming to an end on the Easter weekend. And I attended the Easter Sunday service that weekend feeling overly excited and grateful to the Lord for the time spent in His presence. I went to the Sunday service that weekend without any agenda but to worship the Lord and give Him thanks, so I was totally surprised by what happened next. As I stood worshipping the Lord, the Holy Spirit softly spoke these words to me: "Sasha I want you to tell those demonic spirits residing in you that they have to leave in Jesus' Name!"

The sound of these words surprised me and I could not believe what I was hearing. I had experienced hearing the voice of the Lord on many occasions before, but for some reason this time I chose to disregard it. I carried on worshipping the Lord with everyone else until the Holy Spirit repeated the same words to me again.

By now fear had gripped my heart and I told the Holy Spirit, "I can't do that because I'm scared." The Holy Spirit responded to this by telling me, "When the Pastor Clem gives the invitation for prayer, I want you to go forward and I will set you free." After a lot of reasoning and debating I eventually agreed to do it and waited for the call.

As I waited anxiously for the invitation from Pastor I will never forget what happened next. Another voice began to speak to me also, and it told me that if I made any attempt to go to the front for prayer and deliverance it would embarrass me badly in front of all those people. I will not lie to you — this frightened me a little, so I quietly spoke to the Holy Spirit and told Him that I really did not want to be embarrassed or anything like that, so maybe going down to the front was not a good thing to do after all. At this the Holy Spirit did not answer me, and the other voice continued to speak. "If you go forward for prayer I am going to kill you," was one of the main things I remember it saying to me. And at that point, I became absolutely frozen with fear and my whole body was shaking like a leaf.

To make a long story short the Holy Spirit was spot on, and like He had told me Pastor Clem gave an invitation for anyone who wanted prayer to come out to the front. At first I did not move and stood glued to where I was, listening to the demonic spirit's comments and suggestions. But after a short pause the Holy Spirit gently beckoned for me to come and I did. Honestly, I don't know how I broke through the fear to get down those steps to the front, but I did — I just kept walking!

As I stood in the line and waited for Pastor Clem to get down the prayer line to me, I could hear this demonic voice in my head trying to persuade me to go back to my seat. The voice went from being friendly to being abusive, and the more it spoke to me the more I was determined that I was going to be set free. I remembered standing there calling out the name of Jesus over and over again and repenting for all the times that I had wilfully refused to listen to His counsel.

It seemed like I waited in this prayer line for ages before Pastor Clem got to me, but when he did the Lord used him to set me free in an instant. I had struggled with my issue of sexual sin for so long and could not conquer it alone, but one touch from the Lord and my struggles with the spirits of perversion, pride, and bondage were broken in an instant!

My wise decision to let the Holy Spirit help me with my struggle with sexual sin was probably the main turning point in my whole situation. I say this because although I had gained victory over the devil in other areas of my life, my sexual sin would have always been a restrictive factor in the amount of progress I could have made. Its hold over me would have ultimately hindered and limited the things the Lord wanted to do through me, and I would never have been able to put Him or His Will first.

It was one of the hardest things I have ever had to do, but I am so glad that the Lord gave me the strength to endure and conquer it!

It is a gradual process!

As I look back in reflection over this period of my life, there is one key thing that stands out very clearly to me — from the time that my heart was left broken to the time of my deliverance and healing — *it was a process!* It had been a long, tiring process, and there were times when I would have gladly given up if not for the grace of God!

For every great thing that is accomplished there has to be a gradual process. Even a beautiful rose bush in all its summer splendour had to begin as a small seed! Like a rose, I too had to go through a gradual process from pain to glory, and I must admit that in the beginning I was not very happy about the prospect of having to go through it all, but, today I have come to the conclusion that I would not have wanted it any other way.

In this chapter, I credit my actual breakthrough to the Easter weekend when the Lord set me free, but the truth is that there were many other events and situations that contributed to my healing and deliverance. For example, the day I chose to make the Lord a bigger part of my life, my efforts to read the Word of God more often, my desire to hear the voice of God for myself, my decision to attend a church regularly, my decision to use my authority as a believer, and my decision to do it His Way all played their part in the process and these factors, and many others, contributed to my success in making it through.

I am a person who likes to have things handed to me on a plate, and if I am honest I have been quite spoiled by my friends and family. So when I realised that I would have to go through some kind of long process in order to receive my healing and deliverance, I was not too happy with the Lord. I simply wanted Him to take away my pain and set me free instantly, without any fuss. I did not want to give anything up, learn new ways, go through a five-year process, or basically do any work for my deliverance and healing. For years I could not understand what the Lord's problem was. I think this is probably the reason the Lord chose to take me through the route He did. He obviously knew I had a lot of maturing to do before He could use me for His glory!

There are many highlights and lowlights that I can remember going through on my journey with the Lord, but if I were to narrow them down with the view of encouraging you in three main things that I believe would help your process run much more smoothly than mine, it would be to focus your attention on the Lord, be obedient to Him, and in spite of everything, hold on to the Word of God. I chose these three things to share with you because if I had had someone there to encourage me during my time of need, I would have liked them to have shared these three things with me.

For a long period during my distress, I spent too much time focusing my attention on the problem. I literally did not think about anything other than my situation. I would think about it all the time and when I was not thinking about it of my own accord, I would allow the devil to talk to me about his views and opinions on it. This was undeniably one of the biggest mistakes I made. It not only kept me thinking about a lot of things that were not actually happening it also prevented me from spending these times immersed in the Word and things of God.

If I had simply followed Godly counsel *(see 2 Corinthians 10:5)* and made up my mind to refocus my attention on the Lord, I would have been a lot better off and things would have run a lot more smoothly. I take full responsibility for this mistake because I knew better. I had studied enough Scriptures concerning the subject of controlling my mind to know, and the fact that I was still allowing the devil to have this hold over me was not one of my brighter decisions.

The next piece of advice I would like to share with you is to be obedient to the Lord *(see Deuteronomy 8)*. This was another main reason why I struggled in my process for so long.

If the Word of God says something, and I don't care what it is, you had better do it; you will save yourself a lot of time and effort in the long run. And if you ever find yourself struggling with a particular area you should give it to the Holy Spirit and ask Him to help you with it. Remember, God has given us these "**B**asic **I**nstructions **B**efore **L**eaving **E**arth" to help us live victoriously. He knows all things and is aware of all the pitfalls the devil has planned for our destruction and because He loves us so much, God has freely shared them with us.

I was really disobedient to the Lord during my process. In fact, looking back on the whole episode, I cannot believe the extent of my disobedience. I did not realise it at the time, but part of the reason for my long battle to freedom was definitely caused by my disobedience. If you have found yourself at this junction in your battle, I would strongly encourage you to turn from your disobedience quickly and obey the Holy Spirit completely.

The last piece of wisdom and advice I want to share with you before I close this chapter is this: despite absolutely everything and anything, hold on to the Lord and the Word of God *(see Psalm 42)*.

By now you are probably starting to realise that the process is not necessarily going to be a smooth or easy one. It wasn't for me, and I guess this could possibly be the case for you! From the moment you decide to give up your struggle to the Lord and use your weapon — the Word of God, the devil will fight you all the way to prevent this from happening. The key to your success will depend on your tenacity in holding on to the Lord no matter what. There will be times when you will not see any way out, and even times when you may feel like the Lord has deserted you, but you will have to just hold on and ride it out. I had to do this myself and I am not sharing anything with you that I have not personally experienced first-hand, so I know that holding on to the Lord actually works!

I guarantee you that if you choose to hold on to the Lord and the Word of God, even in the really hard times, He will see you through to the other side *(see Matthew 8:23-27)*. By the grace of God I did not give up my battle and as a result I experienced total freedom and victory. *Do not give up your battle because He truly delivers! He truly heals! He truly restores!*

Chapter Eight

Where do I go from here Lord?

We all need a positive example to follow!

I hope this book has blessed you and that it has helped to answer some of the questions, thoughts, and feelings you may be experiencing in your own situation. When the Lord chose me to write this book, I honestly believe He had you in mind, and that His greatest desire is to see you set free from your pain so you can live the abundant life of blessings and breakthroughs which He came to give us *(Psalm 34:3-5)*.

I did not choose to write this book of my own accord because it is something that I could not have done by my own strength. However, the Lord has fully equipped me and given me the strength to do it for the simple reason that others need to be delivered from their pain before it is too late.

The Lord has allowed me to experience what it is like to be free — free from the bondage of bowing down to what others may think and say about me and my circumstances. The Lord has taught me that His acceptance is all I need for my life, and He has accepted me for whom and what I am, *which is such an awesome feeling*! I no longer allow the opinions of others to govern my life, and it is most definitely a liberating feeling. Once again, I thank You, my Lord!

In writing this book, I believe the Lord wants to use me as a point of contact to reach out to those who feel their struggle is unique. A belief such as this can be so overwhelming and daunting, but I want you to know that it is just one of those tricks that I spoke about in Chapter

Four, a trick of the devil to stop you from getting to the finish line and winning your race. The truth is that there are others going through, and those that have already gone through, this same heartache. Really, you are not alone in this, and if you do not believe me when I say this, look at what the Word of God tells us concerning such things. It is found in 1 Peter 5:9 and reads as follows: *"We should stand firm against him (devil), be strong in your faith. Remember that your Christian brothers and sisters all over the world are going though the same kind of suffering you are"* (NLT).

The Lord is an all-knowing God. He knows our end right from the beginning, and if He has asked me to write this book to help others, I am more than 100 percent confident that it will accomplish a great purpose in the lives of many, because I know that my Lord does not do anything by accident *(1 Thessalonians 2:4)*. For the simple fact that the Spirit of God has led you to this book, I am certain there has been something for you in these pages.

The Lord has encouraged me to share my all with you: the state of my relationship, the thoughts, feelings, and pain I experienced, the hopeless things that I so desperately tried to hold on to, the battle in my mind, and my deliverance and healing process. It has been quite a hard thing for me to do, and I even held back from the Lord for a whole year while I considered if I really wanted to tell my story or not. The Lord is so faithful, loving, and giving, though, and when He kept gently asking me to trust Him and do it, I knew He would empower me with the strength I needed to see the process through to the end.

Through it all, from the beginning of my life to the moment of my distress and right up to this very moment, the Lord has never stopped loving and guiding me. Not only has He helped me get over my pain, He has also helped me get over myself! He helped me in all things, even at a time when I was not aware that it was Him.

Long before I even considered what I would include in this chapter, the Holy Spirit shared with me that He wanted me to dedicate one of the chapters in this book to helping others recognise some of the various avenues of help He has so graciously provided for us. He also told me that, "Where do I go from here Lord?" is a question many people are asking today.

When I was going through my distress and I asked the Holy Spirit this same question, the thought that somebody else may be asking this same question never even occurred to me. So I am quite honoured that the Lord would choose me as a vessel to answer this question for others.

I honestly believe that when you begin to put some of these things I am about to share with you into practice, your healing and deliverance will surely come. As I am writing these words I cannot contain the excitement that has just filled my heart and soul — the excitement of seeing you healed and restored! And as CeCe Winans sings out "Falling in Love" and "Million Miles" in the background, my heart is filled with so much peace and joy (see 1 Peter 1:8).

I am the kind of person that learns things from the examples of others. I like to follow Biblical examples, as well as the positive examples of people around me. Basically, I am prepared to take your advice if you have applied it to your own life and it has worked out for you!

The Word of God says that a good tree cannot produce bad fruits and a bad tree cannot produce good fruits. Therefore, we can identify a good or bad tree by its fruits, and likewise we can identify people by their actions (see Matthew 7:15-20). I usually apply this Biblical truth to my choices and decision-making before choosing to follow someone's example and I would advise you to do the same!

The way the Lord will choose to help you and the way that He chose to help me may differ in some ways, but the fact still remains — He will help you. I say this to you because I do not want to mislead you into thinking that your help and deliverance will happen in the exact way mine did.

On my journey with the Lord there were many times when I felt completely discouraged by the Lord's choice of method for delivering me, and the fact that I could not fully comprehend His Way and timing was extremely hard for me to deal with. As a result, I created a lot of problems for myself.

The reason I mention this is because I feel in my spirit that some of you may still be struggling with the idea of allowing the Lord to have full control of your situation.

Well, speaking from the point of view of someone who the Lord has successfully delivered and healed from a broken-hearted experience, the only advice I can give you is to encourage you to completely trust and obey the Lord, as His Way is perfect! *(See 2 Samuel 22:31).*

As I take you through some of the steps of the process the Holy Spirit took me through in my own search for answers, I want you to ask the Holy Spirit to guide and lead you through your process. I want you to ask Him to show you, teach you, and give you a peace that surpasses all understanding (*Philippians 4:7*), for I know that when you ask, He will hear and do it for you!

About a year ago, when the Holy Spirit first led me to write the outline for this chapter, my belief was that I would present these steps to you in some kind of chronological order. Since then the Holy Spirit shared with me that this was not really necessary, as there is no real importance or reason for someone else to follow my example chronologically. The Holy Spirit told me that the overall purpose for including this chapter was to show others that He has already prepared various avenues to help them in their time of need (*see Psalm 72:12*). And this of course may vary depending on the individual.

For some of you, it may be hard to believe that the Lord would really want to help you with such a situation, and right now, I believe that some of you may be saying to yourselves things like, "But I don't even know the Lord," "Why would He want to help me?" "Can the Lord even help me with my situation?" And, "What have I ever done to deserve help from the Lord?"

Whatever your thoughts, beliefs or questions, the answer is and always will remain the same: *"His faithful love endures forever,"* (see Psalm 136:23-24) and, *". . . there is now no condemnation (no adjudging guilty of wrong) for those who are in Christ Jesus, who live [and] walk after the dictates of the flesh, but after the dictates of the Spirit"* (Romans 8:1 AMP). (Does that answer your questions?)

As you continue to read, I want you to keep the two things I have just mentioned in the forefront of your mind. I would like you to do this because I know first-hand that the devil will now come and try to mess with your mind with the sole purpose of distracting you from experiencing the Lord's love and help. The devil hates it when we turn to the Lord for our help because he knows that the Lord will always step in and deliver us!

At this exact moment, the key is to keep your focus on the Lord. I don't care what pain you are still going to experience from this moment forth, the tears you are going to shed, or even the feeling of not being able to carry on, which I must add will probably get much stronger now than ever before. Just keep your focus on Jesus Christ!

My words may seem a bit unsympathetic to you at this moment in time, but I say them because I know too well what the devil is capable of doing if he can trick us into taking our focus off the Lord and onto our problems and circumstances. They may seem like insensitive words at the moment, but believe me, one day you will thank me for my bluntness.

Remember, everything begins with a decision and you will have to decide whether or not you will work with the Holy Spirit to fight the good fight of faith (*1 Timothy 6:12).*

"But I don't want to fight . . . I do not have any strength left in me to fight . . . I just want to be well again . . . I . . ." I hear someone say. So let me share some home truths with you.

Whether we like it or not we are all involved in a spiritual battle between the Lord and the devil. The Lord wants us and the devil wants to destroy us. God wants us because He loves us and longs to fulfil His divine purpose through us, whereas the devil wants us because he hates us and wants to destroy us. The devil hates the fact that we still have an opportunity for fellowship with God, knowing full-well that he will never have this opportunity again! The bottom line is that the devil is jealous of us and has made it his ultimate goal to destroy as many of us as he possibly can. So, the reality of it all is that we are all involved in this spiritual war whether we like it or not. Many of us have recognised this and have prepared for war, but there are still a lot of us that are in a state of ignorance, refusing to accept reality! (*I pray that you will not be one of the latter ones!*)

My prayer for you is that you will be one of those that say, "Thank you Holy Spirit for giving me this revelation and equipping me for this battle, and because Jesus Christ has already conquered the devil for me at Calvary, I know the outcome of my efforts will always end victoriously."

I know these words that we have just declared are so encouraging, but you must first remember that you will need to have the Lord on your side if you are going to receive this victory, because if He is not on your side, the devil will make mincemeat out of you!

As you have read through the various avenues the Lord made available to me, I want you to take the time to think about them, meditate on them, talk to the Holy Spirit about them, and then eventually, depending on what the Holy Spirit is instructing you to do, begin to apply them to your own situation.

Steps in the right direction

- *You will have to give the Lord your consent to heal your broken heart and work together with Him.*

Now, I am not in any doubt that the Lord can heal your broken heart, but I must warn you that it is going to be a two-way process and one that will require your participation. Like I have mentioned before, the Lord will not go against your own free will. If you are happy to stay in your condition the Lord's hands will be tied. It will not matter how much the Lord wants to help you get through your situation, if you don't want His help, He will not force it upon you. It will break His heart to see you hurting and in so much pain, but there will be nothing He can do.

Here is a following analogy on this matter and I hope it will help you to see this thing more clearly: If you set off with the intentions of going to work one morning and you just sit in your car, but you do not make the decision to use your key to start the engine — it does not take a genius to realise that the car will not be able to take you to work. It will not matter how reliable and faithful the car is in getting you to work, the fact will still remain — the car will not move. When it boils down to it, it is going to be your decisions and actions that will determine whether or not that car will move!

I really hope that this illustration has made this point clearer to you: *God needs our cooperation!*

"But God has the power to do all things!" I hear someone say. And yes, you are right — God does have the power to do all things and make all things happen, but it is also true that God is a Spirit and spirits need a cooperative physical body to operate in this physical (earthly) realm.

- **Seek to find God's divine purpose for your life and then work towards it.**

Many of us spend most of our time going through life without any real plans or purpose, and it is as though we are walking through life with a big black bag over our heads trying desperately to get to our destinations. Of course, this is impossible to do because we cannot see where we are going or what we are doing, but for some reason most of us are still not fazed by this and are happy to plod along in the same old state for years.

Whether we like it or not we all need some kind of purpose for our lives because it gives us a valuable reason for doing what we are doing. A singer's purpose is to make good music that other people will listen to and be inspired by. An author's purpose is to write books that others will enjoy reading, a teacher's purpose is to pass on valuable knowledge and information that others can benefit from, and a football player's purpose is to work as part of a team to score goals in order to win a football match or tournament.

Some people recognise their purpose at a young age, and then there are some that will not recognise it until they are much older. Some people recognise their purpose on their own and then there are some, like me, who only recognise it when they come into relationship with the Lord.

I spent a lot of my early years going through life without any real purpose, and the purpose I had initially set for myself was quite negative and limited. As a young teenager, I simply flittered from one thing to another, depending on how I felt or what was fashionable at the time.

When I came to know the Lord, I realised very quickly that He had a plan and purpose for us all *(see Romans 9:11)*, and it was quite a relief for me to know this. I would hear others talk about God's plan and purpose for the ones that He calls His own all the time, so I decided to ask the Holy Spirit what His purpose was for me. Why not? I thought to myself, *It was not as if I had had any real plans of my own.*

To have any kind of positive purpose is a good thing for anyone, but to know God's divine purpose for your life is an even greater thing!

When I was at university training to become a teacher, I used to think that once I had finished my degree and had started teaching I would be happy, content, and complete. And although I was right to a certain extent, this sense of contentment and fulfilment only stayed with me for a short while before I began to feel like something else was missing. As much as I love being in the classroom, working with young children, my passion for being there just wasn't the same after awhile. To begin with, I was so sure that teaching young children was all I wanted to do with my life, but as time went on and I developed my relationship with the Lord, the purpose that I initially chose for myself didn't seem that fulfilling anymore. Recently I have come to the conclusion that the only real satisfaction I am ever going to experience is when I am walking in God's divine purpose and doing His will for my life.

I often hear people say things like, "Life is what you make it!" And I don't really think anything more of it, but this saying is so true.

I am aware that many of you may have your own big intentions and purposes for your life — and this is a good thing — but I would like to suggest and encourage you to find out what God's purpose is for your life. Not only will it be much bigger and more fulfilling than what you could possibly think or achieve for yourself, it will also give you a greater sense of peace, contentment, and fulfilment, one that will not leave you feeling empty after you have finished chasing it down!

- ***Renew your mind regularly with the Word of God*** - *use and meditate on Scriptures that apply to your situations, thoughts, and feelings.*

"Instead, let the Spirit renew your thoughts and attitudes" Ephesians 4:23 (NLT).

In Chapter Six, I discussed how important it is for you to get a grip on your mind. I also shared with you that the mind is the place where the devil wages his greatest war against us.

The devil is not silly, he knows that if we do not have control over our minds, we will not be able to reject and cast down the negative thoughts and images he is continuously trying to inject into them. The devil knows too well that if we allow him to have control over our minds, there is absolutely nothing we can do to pull ourselves out of our depression and painful state.

The devil had me in a corner for a long time because I would not take heed of God's counsel and control my thoughts. He badgered me to a point near death and would have possibly killed me had it not been for the Lord's intervention.

It is a good thing the Lord does not allow us to go through more than we can bear *(1 Corinthians 10:13)* or else I don't know what I would have done.

The more you continue to cry out to the Lord and seek to learn His Way, the more He is able to empower you and give you the strength needed to overcome your situation.

Like I said before, the Holy Spirit led me to the book *Battlefield of the Mind* by Joyce Meyer, and it was a result of reading this book that the Lord was able to enlighten me about the issues I was experiencing. My mindset had been wrong for so long that I just assumed that my mind and thinking were the way they were supposed to be.

After reading Meyer's book, I still had a long way to go in gaining control of my mind, but at least this new revelation shed some new light on my situation and opened up my spiritual eyes to certain things that I was experiencing. It helped me realise that I would have to actually ask the Holy Spirit to help me with my battle against the devil. I know the devil was mad when I got this revelation because he knew that once I finally realised I could win my battle by rejecting certain thoughts and choosing to replace them with the Word and thoughts of God, I would eventually gain back full control over my mind and he would no longer hold sway over me.

Using the concepts in Joyce Meyer's book also helped me realise I would have to read the Bible more and listen to Godly counsel concerning my situation. I did not realise it until then, but it is the Word of God that renews our minds and helps to set us free, so I would strongly recommend that you read it, study it, and meditate on it! And trust me; it is only when you do this that you will begin to be victorious over the devil in every area of your life!

- **Control and train your mind** – *not every thought you have should be meditated or acted upon!*

I have already discussed the subject of controlling your mind in my previous point, but for the mere fact that I initially recorded it twice, I will again stress its importance — *Take back control of your mind!*

You do not have to meditate on or give in to every thought that may come into your head. If the thought or action does not help you in any way, reject it! If it makes you feel worse than you already do, reject it! If it is an image that you just don't need to see, reject it! If it does not line up with the Word of God, reject it! And while you are rejecting them make sure you have a relevant Scripture on hand that you can use to meditate on in the place of these negative thoughts and images. This is something you will have to do for yourself but don't worry, the Holy Spirit will give you the power and strength that you need to do it:

"That's why I take pleasure in my weaknesses, and in the insults, hardships, persecutions, and troubles that I suffer for Christ. For when I am weak, then I am strong" (2 Corinthians 12:10, NLT).

In fact, from this moment on, until you see victory in you situation, I want you to declare this out loud: *"Devil, your time is up because I am taking back full control of my mind!"*

- **Godly counsel and guidance is extremely important** – *but you must also remember that such counsel must also line up with the Word of God!*

Are you familiar with the saying "No man is an island"? Well, I first heard this saying on a record many years ago. At the time I was not really sure of its meaning, but I am now!

For me, I believe this phrase simply means that we all need somebody at some point or another in our lives. We can not possibly live alone! Some of us may think that we don't need others because we have everything under control and that we can happily live on our own without interaction with other people. But the truth is that we all really do need the company and help of others in order to function in the way that God intended. Even God, with all His wisdom, knew that it would not be good for Adam to be alone without the companionship of a woman, Eve.

I believe there are three main sources that will influence our choice of friends and relationships we choose to get involved in. There are relationships chosen for us by the Lord, the relationships we choose for ourselves, and the relationships the devil chooses for us. Would you agree?

The friendships and relationships that are influenced by the devil are usually the ones that will keep us so busy compromising God's will for our lives that we will never really be able to experience the fullness of the Lord's love, plan, and purpose for our lives. These relationships are completely unproductive!

Next we have the friendships and relationships we choose for ourselves using our own judgment and criteria. In this case, the chances of selecting a really good friend is 50/50 and on occasions where your judgment has not been so great there is even a possibility that you may reap the same problems as the friendships and relationships chosen for you by the devil. (Like for example, the relationship that left me broken-hearted.)

Finally, we have the friendships and relationships God ordained for us — the most imperative one of the three! God's influence is undeniably the most important of all three sources because this is the one that will ensure we achieve our maximum potential in God's ultimate plan for our life.

As a result of trusting the Lord, I made a conscious decision to seek more Godly friendships and relationships. Don't get me wrong, I haven't turned my back on my friends I knew before I came to the Lord, and I still sometimes choose some of my own new friends now, but the difference now is that I have an awareness of the boundaries that God has set for such relationships. For example, I will not hesitate to override or disregard the advice of a good friend if what they are saying to me does not line up with the Word of God or with what the Holy Spirit is saying to me.

"Some people say," you might object, "that you will only really know who your true friends are when you are down on your face!" And I will add to this by saying, "When you are on your face you will definitely see who will stand by you and who will not." (I certainly experienced this truth first-hand!)

To be honest with you, in a way I knew beforehand the ones that would stand by me and the ones that would not, but it still hurts when you know that you would have been there for them in their real time of need and they were not there for you.

I can think of a handful of friends that were really there for me, friends that would speak to me for hours when I really needed to escape from my torment, but there was one friend in particular that was there for me big time. This particular friend was definitely one of those God-sent friends I spoke of before. She was there to pray with me at any time of day or night and she encouraged me, listened to me, heard my cries, loved me and my son, taught me the Word of God and how to cling to Him in my time of need, visited me at my home, and she also made her home available to me. She was a total blessing to me and even now I truly thank the Lord for her life!

The fact that she loved the Lord, His Way and His Word was such a blessing to me, and it really encouraged me to develop a more meaningful relationship with Him.

I believe that we all need a friend like this, especially when we are going through hard times, and so I want to encourage you to ask the Holy

Spirit to speak to your heart and reveal to you who your true God-sent friends are. This will definitely help you in your time of need.

One of the requirements that I want you to look out for when you are choosing these particular friends is that he or she is spiritually stronger and more mature than you. I say this because when you are at your lowest point, it is always a good idea to hang with others that can strengthen you and lift you up. It is a time when you will really need to hear from the Lord and not just a friend!

- **Attend church regularly** - *a church where they deal with real life issues and apply Biblical principles and truths.*

My advice to you, if you are not already in a Holy Bible-based church, is to pray and ask the Holy Spirit to lead you to a church that believes that Jesus Christ is our Lord and Saviour.

I have heard many people say that you don't have to go to a church to love God or to have Him in your heart, and this is true to a certain extent, but let us also remember the Bible tells us that Christians should fellowship with one another regularly and help to build each other up in the faith (*Hebrews 10:25*).

During the time of my distress, God seemed so far away to reach. This was not because He actually was. It was more a case in which I was far away from Him. This occurred because of lack of knowledge, and lack of knowledge occurred because I did not read my Bible! My thinking at that time was, "Lord, I spend a lot of time crying out to you, and I go to church occasionally so why won't you help me?" I just could not understand why I felt like the Lord was too far for me to reach. And when others used to suggest to me that I should try attending church more regularly in order to hear the Word of God being taught and preached, I did not really think this would help.

When I first became a Christian, I did not like church that much. Every church service I went to would talk about living a holy life and having faith in the Lord, and most of the time it all went over my head because I was not ready to live a holy life or fully trust the Lord. Saying that, there were other times when I would really enjoy a church service, but after the touching moments had finished and I would get home, I could not help but think that the Lord's Way was impossible and could not really help me with my real life issues.

When I say issues, I am speaking of issues such as how it is all fine and well that the preacher stood there and told me that I should not be having sex out of marriage, but how would I go about stopping such a thing, if I really did not want to? Would the Lord still love me then? The issues I was experiencing at the time made me feel like such a hypocrite, and for this reason I felt that I could not really commit myself to a church.

Feeling like a hypocrite is another trick orchestrated by the devil to prevent you from going to church and hearing Biblical truths that will eventually set you free — so don't fall for it!

The day the Holy Spirit led me to the particular church I went to during this period of my life was a total blessing for me. It was at this church that I was taught how to apply the Word of God to real life issues. I learned various Biblical principles and truths such as how to develop my self-confidence, worth, and esteem; how to become a Godly woman with Godly values and principles; how to give my first to God; the reasons why God would want me to live a certain way; and how to give and show Godly love to others. I learned so much at this church and I truly thank the Lord for leading me there in my time of need.

If you are not already a member of a church, I would like to encourage you to ask the Holy Spirit to lead you to the place where He wants you to be, a place where you will grow!

Just ask Him, believe Him and trust Him and He will do the rest. He will lead you to the place where He wants you to be.

- ***Find the time to get in God's presence and talk to Him*** - *Learn to hear and distinguish God's voice for yourself.*

When you are alone and there is no one else around is usually when the devil and those other little voices will come to further distress you. I know this well because the devil would most often attack me when I was alone.

The devil knows that if he can get you to a point where you cannot face the world, he will have you in a corner where you will not have much room to manoeuvre. Picture this: it is like watching a boxing match when one competitor gets his opponent into a corner and is able to unleash blow after blow on him. There is a right time for everything (Ecclesiastes 3) and being on your own is not really a bad thing, but it can be in these circumstances!

Now, I know everyone has their own life to get on with, and I know that we should not be totally dependent on other people because they can let us down, but do you know that when you are physically alone, you are not really by yourself? If you are a believer, you have the presence of the Holy Spirit residing with you, waiting patiently for you to invite Him into all your life situations *(see 2 Corinthians 13:14)*. Friends are important, but you cannot depend solely on them the way you can depend on the Lord.

The Lord loves it when we put Him first in all aspects of our lives. He also loves it when we come to Him for all that we need because only He alone can fill our souls *(see Psalms 107:9)*.

Since I am a quick learner it didn't take long for me to realise that the lonely periods would eventually have to come at the end of each day. I also learned very quickly that the devil would make his way over to my house to torment me in the evenings. I hated these times so much because I knew the devil's reasons for showing up, and the fact that I hated being in the presence of the enemy eventually pushed me into seeking the presence of the Lord more and more. As a direct result, I learned to converse with the Holy Spirit about everything imaginable. I learned to sit alone in His presence and pour out my heart to Him, and guess what? I found it to be more peaceful and helpful than anything I had ever experienced or known!

- *Keep a simple daily diary of your days* – *not only will it help you during the process, it will also help you recall things later on that may help someone else.*

I am a person that likes to write things down for reflection and future reference, so you will always find me writing notes. I cannot remember when or why I learned to do this, but I started to keep journals of my day-to-day life when I began attending the church that taught me so much. I started off by keeping notes of the church services and this progressed to recording key things that had happened to me on a daily basis, the things that the Holy Spirit shared with me, and eventually the outline for this book.

The notes I have kept over the years have been very useful to me and my walk with the Lord and towards my destiny because without them I would have possibly forgotten many of the key events that led me to the place I am today. I keep record of my thoughts, my conversations, my feelings, my failures, and my accomplishments, and from time to time I sit down and get all my journals out and read through the things I have experienced over the years. There are things in my journals that the Lord shared with me years ago, things I can actually see manifesting in my life today.

Keeping these journals has not only allowed me to reflect on many things, it has also allowed me to see how faithful the Lord has been to me over the years. As I look back on the things the Lord first shared with me years ago, I can now see them manifesting in my life. It gives me an unspeakable joy and great pleasure to see and know that God is really true to His Word and has the ability to carry out what He says He will if I do my part and trust and obey Him. (*See Isaiah 55:11*).

I would like to encourage you to keep a written record, a simple account detailing what you have experienced, for the sole purpose that you will have something to refer back to in your time of need. It is a bit like snapshots of your life that you can look back on from time to time to see how you have progressed and grown. (See Habakkuk 2:2-4). I know that it is not something for everyone and some people do not like this method of recording, but you will not really know whether or not it is for you unless you give it a try. So I challenge you to try it out and see how it goes for a little while before you cross the idea off completely. And who knows, you may completely shock yourself and actually like it!

Imagine if what you once recorded, as nothing more than merely keeping a personal record for yourself, soon became the advice and answer to someone else's problems. It's not impossible, look what happened to me!

- ***Ask the Holy Spirit to help you overcome and break bad habits and strongholds*** - *ask Him to help you kill your flesh.*

Now, there are some things we can do by our own strength, and these things can even help us achieve great things in our lives, but we must still remember that there are also some things that we will never be able to do with our own strength and power.

It will be up to you to discern the things that you just cannot achieve or do with your own strength and ask the Holy Spirit to help you to conquer or accomplish them. In fact, I would suggest that you ask the Holy Spirit to help you surrender all areas of your life to Him, so that He can take you to places and show you things you would never experience without Him *(see John 14:26)*.

Jesus tells us in John 14:26 that He would have to go back to His Father for awhile, but that in His absence He would send us the Holy Spirit to help us in all things. If you believe this and accept that the Holy Spirit is now here on earth and helping us with our lives, then I would strongly recommend today that you begin to give all those personal challenges to the Lord and ask Him help you conquer them. I want you to remember that there is no condemnation in Christ Jesus and God is not judging us, so it does not matter what those things are that you are struggling with, just confess them and give them over to Him to make right.

This is a time when you will have to be honest and tell God the absolute truth about the way you are feeling and thinking, such as not really wanting to give up the man that is actually causing you so much pain or the fact that you may not yet be at a stage where you totally trust God. This is fine and the Lord is not put off by such things. He is more concerned with showing you His love and the condition of your heart than He is with the way you may be feeling emotionally in your time of distress.

I know this from first-hand experience because I cried out to the Lord in my state of total distress, confusion, sin, and pain and He still came to my rescue. Like I said before, I used to tell the Holy Spirit straight that I would do anything He told me to do in order to get me through my pain, apart from giving up this man. I listened to the Holy Spirit for years and even followed many of His instructions, but I still refused to give up this man when I was told to.

The point I am trying to make is that the Lord still stuck by me through all of this, and He still helped me through to the other side.

Really, there are some bad habits and strongholds that can only be broken by the power of God, and the devil knows this. That is why he does not want us to ask the Lord to help us break them. The devil tries to trick us into thinking that we cannot possibly share such sinful things with God or even ask Him to help us with them because God hates sin. Well the only truth in this trick from the devil is that God hates sin, the rest of it is all a lie. The devil knows full well that we need the Lord's help to conquer the power that sin has over us, and he also knows too well that when we ask the Lord to help us conquer our sin the Lord will happily do it for us.

Let me leave you with this: *never stop confessing your sin and being truthful with the Lord!*

- ***Be prepared to give some things up*** *– some things you may not really want to give up, especially those things that don't line up with the Word and character of God.*

I could sit here and tell you that the Lord will not expect you to give up anything, but I don't see the point in lying to you. After all, you will probably come to this realisation at some point so you might as well hear it now. As you get more and more intimate with the Lord and your relationship begins to grow, there will be some things the Holy Spirit will ask you to sacrifice for your own good.

The Lord wants you to put Him first in every area of your life. He wants to be your first love, first in your heart, first in your mind, first in your finances, first in your family, first in your career, first in your workplace, and like I said before, He basically just wants to be first in absolutely every area of your life!

Putting the Lord first in your life is probably the biggest sacrifice of all we will ever have to make. You could possibly place it on the same level as what Abraham had to endure when God requested that he sacrifice his long-awaited son Isaac on the altar as a burnt offering in Genesis Chapter 22. Although God eventually stopped Abraham from actually going ahead with it, I believe that He simply asked this of Abraham to see if he would really put Him first before anything — even his own son! I really do thank the Lord that He did not ask such a big sacrifice of me in the beginning because I would have not have been able to do it.

For me, and it will probably be the same with you, the Lord allowed me to continue in a way I felt comfortable with to allow me time to build up my trust in Him. The Lord knew that I would have to develop my trust in Him before I could totally surrender my life to Him. So for this reason, He did not ask me to sacrifice anything in the beginning.

He just listened to my cries, taught me His Ways and allowed me to experience an unconditional love I had never experienced before.

As time went on, I simply fell in love with the Lord and started to trust Him more and more, and before I knew it, I began to make sacrifices for the Lord of my own accord. He has never and will never force me to sacrifice anything. I have simply come to a point in my relationship with Him where I choose to sacrifice certain things of my own accord because I know and understand why He has asked me to refrain from them. The Lord has and continues to prove Himself to me time and time again, and it is this reason alone why I choose to worship Him the way I do!

At this point I would like to encourage you to go before the Lord and ask Him to reveal to you all the things that are hindering your progress. You may not want to give them up right now, but at least if you are aware of them when you do decide that you are ready to sacrifice them you will know what they are!

- ***Be honest with the Holy Spirit about your thoughts and feelings towards Him and those involved in your situation*** *– you will only be lying to yourself if you are not!*

Again, I have to say that one of the keys to your breakthrough will be your honesty with the Lord. I have touched on this subject before but this time I want to shed more light on being honest with the Holy Spirit in relation to the people involved in your situation.

When I first got into my predicament I did not really know the Lord or His Ways, so I would approach Him about my subject with a holier-than thou attitude — it was so fake! I would share my negative thoughts and feelings about the other people involved in my situation with my friends, but I would never go to the Lord with them. I did not want the Lord to think that I was an awful person. I believed that if I had been honest about this and told the Lord the truth about how I was feeling towards those individuals, the Lord would have been disappointed with me and would possibly not want to help me. I was aware that He could hear me when I was discussing my situation with others but this was fine, as long as I did not speak directly to Him about them.

As a result of not being quite straight with the Lord, I left the door wide open for the devil to use this against me — and of course he entered in through it. The devil would constantly say things to me like, "Christians don't behave like this," "You're not a real Christian," "Do you think that the Lord would help you if He knew your true feelings towards…?" and so on.

For a long while I listened to and believed the devil's suggestions and comments until one day when I could not take it anymore, I declared to the Lord, "If you are going to love me, you are going to have to take me the way I am because I can't pretend anymore." I did not want to pretend anymore, I could not pretend anymore, and more than anything, I just wanted to be free!

This stance turned out to be one of those life-changing moments for me because the Lord did just that. He loved me for who and what I was at that time, and better still, He showed me who and what I was going to become. The truth is that if you are trying to fix yourself up before you come to the Lord, it will never happen!

I would like to encourage you to take off your masks and be yourself with the Lord because this is what He wants more than anything . . . *He loves you for you*!

- *Find out what the Word of God says about you, who you are in Christ and what your inheritance is in Him* — *this is very important because it is the complete truth.*

Before I was left devastated by the breakup of my relationship, I held quite a high opinion of myself. I was confident, fun to be around, exciting, happy, determined, persistent, cheeky, and I certainly had some high hopes for myself. So it came as a big surprise, even to me, that after it all happened I began to use words to describe myself as ugly, low self-esteem, lack of confidence, low self-worth and needy.

I had been so sure of my own faith and abilities that if someone had predicted to me that one day I would be left so broken-hearted by a man that I would lose my self-confidence and my desire to live, I would never have believed them.

Many of us make the mistake of believing in our own hype. We think we are invincible and that nothing will ever be able to make us change, but the truth is that change is inevitable. In fact, there is only one thing that is unchangeable and that is the Word of God (*Matthew 24:35 & Mark 13:31*). And for this reason, we should not hold on to anything so tightly — that is anything apart from the Word of God!

When I became disillusioned by my own abilities and belief in myself, the Holy Spirit led me to Scriptures that helped me see who and what I really am in Christ, what authority I have in Christ, and my inheritance as a believer. Finding this out helped me see who I really am, and the best thing is that they are all positive. The revelations that I received from these facts allowed me to see myself in a positive light again because if the all-knowing God would say these nice encouraging things about me, why would I choose to believe any differently?

The day I made up my mind to trust God's Word and opinions of me is the day I received a great breakthrough in my life — a break from low self-esteem, low self-worth, lack of confidence and unnecessary pain!

I would strongly like to encourage you to search through the Word of God to find the things that He says you are and have. Not only will you enjoy reading them and knowing that they do really exist, but you will also delight in the fact that God has called you to be a partaker of such great things!

- ***Learn to praise and worship the Lord with all your heart** – Psalms 100*

"Enter into His gates with thanksgiving, and into His courts with praise: be thankful unto Him, and bless His name" (Psalms 100:4, KJV.)

The art of praising and worshipping the Lord in song and through music comes really natural to me, as I have always been a lover of music. I just love to listen to music and sing my heart out to the Lord.

From as young as I can remember, I have always enjoyed and loved listening to music. (Ask anyone that knows me and they will tell you.) The music I really enjoy listening to is usually music that has the ability to touch and inspire me — it has to touch my heart and soul and take me on a journey!

My passion for music, coupled with the fact that I have always known that music has the power to touch and heal the heart and soul, was very beneficial to me during the time of my distress, and when I did reach an all-time low, I naturally turned to music for my help, relief and escape.

I started off by listening to songs that would minister to my need and present state, songs that would encourage me to continue believing because my life was in the hands of the Lord. I then progressed to listening to songs of thanksgiving and praise of the Lord because they seemed appropriate and reflected my gratitude for what He was doing in my life. And eventually I got to the stage where I just wanted to sit in the Lord's presence and worship Him for who He is. *I love worshipping the Lord with my voice, heart and soul!*

It was not until a few years into my battle with this issue that I got the revelation that praise and worship were actually spiritual weapons *(read Joshua 6)*. Until then I was totally ignorant to the fact that I could actually use them to get through challenging situations. But after getting this new revelation I decided that since I was naturally good at it, I would use it against the devil. So I began to learn the art of praising and worshiping the Lord through music, by using my voice, heart and soul.

Praise and worship are powerful spiritual weapons, and are even more powerful when we choose to use them in times when it looks like everything that could possibly go wrong will go wrong. In the really challenging times when I could not focus my attention on reading my Bible or talking to the Lord, the one thing I always seemed to have the strength and ability to do was sing praises and worship to the Lord. It is definitely something we can all do because even when we are doing other things we can still sing praises to and worship the Lord, or simply listen to someone else sing praise and worship to the Lord on your behalf.

I would strongly encourage you to ask the Holy Spirit to teach you how to worship the Lord with all your heart and in spirit and truth (*see John 4:24*). It will surely bless you.

- ***Take one day at a time*** *– with the total assurance that you will come through because nothing is impossible for God.*

On your journey through pain to complete healing and restoration, I want you to take one day at a time. I want you to know that as long as the Lord is on your side you will come out victorious (*Romans 8:37*), so there is no need to rush ahead of the Holy Spirit and mess things up. Each day will bring enough challenges and highlights of its own, and so the best thing for you to do is focus your attention on the day at hand.

On my journey I wanted to know the final outcome from the beginning. There were times when I got so anxious about it all that it only frustrated me and made me feel a hundred times worse than I felt to begin with. I had to learn that in everything there is a process, and that some processes may take longer than others. *(See James 5:7).*

When I think about the term 'process', I cannot help but think about the long process that gold has to go through in order for it to come out at its purest and finest form. The truth is that you will have to go through some uncomfortable things if you are to come out fine and pure. You may have to take some shots, you may fall down a couple of times, and you may even go through many very dark moments when you will ask, "Where are you Lord?" But if you stand on the Word of

God and have faith in Him, you will surely come through (*see Ephesians 6:13*).

Again, I would like to encourage you to take each day one at a time and to spend all of them in the presence of the Lord. *Take each day on its own, knowing that you will come through because there is nothing impossible for God! (See Luke 1:37)*

- **And finally, "Put on the whole Armour of God!"** – *Ephesians 6:13-17*

"Finally, my brethren, be strong in the Lord, and in the power of his might. Put on the whole armour of God, that ye may be able to stand against the wiles of the devil. For we wrestle not against flesh and blood, but against principalities, against powers, against the ruler of the darkness of this world, against spiritual wickedness in high places. Wherefore take unto you the whole armour of God, that you may be able to withstand in the evil day, and having done all, to stand. Stand therefore having your loins girt about with truth, and having on the breastplate of righteousness; And your feet shod with the preparation of the gospel of peace; Above all, taking the shield of faith, where-with ye shall be able to quench all the fiery darts of the wicked. And take the helmet of salvation, and the sword of the Spirit, which is the word of God: praying always with all prayer and supplication in the Spirit, and watching thereunto with all perseverance and supplication for all saints;"
(Ephesians 6:10-18, KJV)

Before I close this chapter there is just one last thing that I would like to encourage you to do: *put on the whole armour of God!*

The armour of God is the spiritual armour the apostle Paul spoke of in the book of Ephesians, the amour that God has freely given to every believer. It is the spiritual armour that we are supposed to put on daily in order to withstand the attacks of the devil. It is in our best interests that we wear it, as we cannot possibly fight the devil with our natural strength and abilities because the "warfare that we experience daily is spiritual; and we cannot fight spiritual things with our natural flesh!" (*2 Corinthians 10:4*). So let us be wise soldiers of Christ and put on:

o *The Helmet of Salvation*

We must always remember our salvation. Jesus died on the cross to save us from our sins and give us eternal life. So this ultimate sacrifice should always be at the fore-front of our minds. We must always keep our focus on Jesus and His promise of eternal life because He is our light and salvation (Psalm 27).

o *The Breastplate of Righteousness*

Your Breastplate of Righteousness is designed to protect your heart and other vital organs. The Word of God tells us that out of the abundance of the heart the mouth speaks (Luke 6:45) and we should guard our heart (Psalm 4:23) because out of it flows the issues of life.

The devil attacks the heart with things such as condemnation and lies because he wants to try and get us to confess negative words over our situations — he wants to grip our hearts with fear. The devil knows that once we begin to confess negative words about what we think, feel, or see we will be held accountable for these words and eventually reap the harvest of what we sow with our mouth. Don't fall for this! Put on the Breastplate of Righteousness and ask the Holy Spirit to help you make the decisions that will enable you to live a pure, righteous, and holy life.

o *The Belt of Truth*

Your Belt of Truth is the source that holds your entire armour together. The Belt of Truth is our Lord and Saviour, Jesus!

Jesus is the Truth that holds our entire spiritual armour together. Jesus is the way, **the truth**, and the life! (John 14:6).

o *Your Feet Shod*

As a Christian (a believer of Jesus Christ) we should always be prepared and ready to spread the good news about Jesus. Wherever we go we should be ready to preach the gospel of peace and share our testimonies. Also, we must let our lifestyle, attitudes, behaviour, and words glorify CHRIST so that others can see Him through us!

○ *Take up the Shield of Faith*

Your Shield of Faith is designed to protect you from the flaming arrows and missiles that the devil throws at us. The devil attacks our minds and our thoughts. This is done to get us to believe and confess the wrong things. If we allow these thoughts and mindsets to linger too long and take focus off the author and finisher of our faith (Hebrews 12:2) we will begin to lose our faith in God.

Don't let your Shield of Faith slip!

○ *And the Sword of the Spirit*

The Word of God (Bible) is your Sword of the Spirit. When the enemy attacks or tempts us we must use the Word of God to defend ourselves against him. Jesus is our ultimate example and he spoke the Word when the devil tried to tempt him in Luke Chapter 4, so we must do the same.

The Sword of the Spirit is sharper than any double-edged sword (Hebrews 4:12). And it is essential that you take up this sword — by learning, meditating, and studying the Word of God — and use it!

Now before I end this chapter, let me leave you with this question to think about. *"When was the last time you saw a soldier in a war zone without his or her armour or weapons?"*

Bonus Chapter!

The Holy Spirit asked me to write this book, which details the fullness of my testimony, in order to encourage others experiencing similar things to trust in Him for help. Although sharing this personal experience with you has been very challenging at times — and I never thought I would say this — I have enjoyed the entire experience immensely.

As the end drew near on this assignment and I had almost completed this book, it was very important to me that I finished it well. After seeking the Holy Spirit for any suggestions on how to end this book, He suggested to me that I should share one last thing with you in closing.

This last thing I am going to share with you is not something I really had to do, and I am quite sure the Lord would have understood if I had decided against it, but it is actually something that I would like to do. I choose to do it because I now have a peace which surpasses all understanding, and I am totally free from this whole affair!

At the start of writing this book, I decided in my heart that I would be as open and honest with you as I possibly could be, but like all good intentions, things don't always go according to plan. The truth is, I have experienced many occasions where I got cold feet about it all, and there were times when I honestly felt like abandoning the whole thing. However, I am thankful that the Lord is truly faithful to His Word (see Hebrews 11:33-34) and has given me the power and strength to stand.

My initial decision to be open and honest with you has occasionally left me asking myself the question, "Are you really sure you want to do this?" I am not going to lie to you, it has been the Holy Spirit's continuous support and guidance through this process that has allowed me to keep my promise to you.

". . . the Comforter (Counselor, Helper, Intercessor, Advocate, Strengthener, Standby), the Holy Spirit, Whom the Father will send in My name [in My place, to represent Me and act on My behalf], He will teach you all things. And He will cause you to recall (will remind you of, bring to your remembrance) everything I have told you."

John 14:26, AMP

I share this Scripture with you because I want you all to know that the Holy Spirit truly is my comforter, my helper, my guider, my teacher, and my advocator!

On my journey from heartbreak to total restoration I have gained so much wisdom from my situation, and if I had to sum it all up in a few words and leave you with one valuable piece of insight that I have learnt about the Lord from my whole experience, it would be this: the Lord is able to meet you at your point of need, in your imperfect state, and is able to heal and restore your broken heart!

Trust me if the Lord can do it for someone like me, there is absolutely no need for you to worry or doubt Him!

A little extra!

On many CDs and DVDs, bonus songs and extra footage are included as a way of giving the buyer a little something extra for purchasing the product. If you enjoy music and buy a lot of CDs like I do, you will probably be familiar with this kind of promotion, and I am sure you would agree that at times this little extra can be quite worthwhile.

One evening as I was talking with the Holy Spirit about the direction of this final chapter, it came to mind that I could use this same notion of a bonus as a means to share the last piece of my testimony with you. I have decided to call this chapter "Bonus Chapter!" because that is simply what it is — a bonus!

Like I said before, this chapter is something that I have chosen to share with you by choice. This book could have ended without it, and you would never have known the difference. The only problem is that I would have known the truth and I would have felt as though I had forfeited my promise to be open and honest with you. I have thought about it quite a bit and I really do believe that this extra revelation is an important part of my testimony. It will bless you.

Unlike the extended amount of time it took me to decide whether or not I would share my heart with you in this book, my decision to share this final revelation took no time at all. When the Holy Spirit suggested that I should share it, straight away I replied, "I will do it." Apart from the fact that I totally trust the Lord with my whole life, and would like to believe that I would do all that I could for Him, I have always admired and appreciated real people who are not afraid to openly share things with others, especially when their motives are to encourage and benefit others.

Since becoming a Christian, I have come across many types of Christian people and were it not for what I would call "real Christians", I would probably have given up my walk with the Lord a long time ago. Such people have taught me that it is OK to be yourself and be real with the Lord, and I truly believe that it is their example that has influenced the position that I am in today — *totally in love with my Lord and Saviour Jesus Christ!*

When the Holy Spirit first instructed me to write this book, it did not occur to me that He would use this opportunity to completely heal and restore my heart and soul, or even that my obedience to follow this instruction would give me complete victory over my situation.

When I first began to write this book my initial belief was that the Lord just wanted to use my testimony to help others overcome similar situations. Never once did I imagine that by writing this book about my own personal experience the Lord could have blessed me in the way that He has done!

By faith!

"Now faith is the confidence that we have what we hope for will actually happen; it gives us the assurance about things we cannot see."

Hebrews 11:1, NLT

I began to write this book in April 2007, after the Holy Spirit instructed me to do so. I was not sure what I was doing. I did not have any real plans in place, and I had never written a book before. I was a complete novice. My instruction from the Holy Spirit was the only thing I had to go on, so I just took each day as it came and waited for Him to guide me through the process. As I waited on the Lord for my further directions and instructions, the Holy Spirit slowly began to direct my paths and before I knew it I was on my way to writing my first book for the Lord.

After a couple of months, when the excitement of implementing such a great task for the Lord had worn off, I debated with myself as to whether or not I was ready to openly share this testimony with others. There was a part of me that wanted to believe that I was ready, because the Holy Spirit told me that He was ready to use my testimony and I really wanted to please Him, but, on the other hand, as I began to remember all the painful memories, the whole thing seemed like more of a challenge than I had thought it would be. It seemed like the more I tried to relive and share those painful memories, the more I became upset about what I was writing. So, after a few months I came to a decision that maybe writing a book for others to read was not a good idea after all, and in June 2007, I eventually stopped writing altogether.

All in all, I held back from writing this book for about a year, and although I knew in my heart that I would finish it someday, at this particular time I did not feel ready to proceed with it.

For the next year thoughts of finishing this book would come to my mind regularly but I would make up excuses to the Holy Spirit as to why it was not a good idea to follow it through. My friends and family who I had shared my intentions with concerning the book would also ask me how it was coming along and I did not have the heart to tell them that I had decided against doing it, so my response to them was to play it down and say that everything was going well.

Around May 2008, I began to reflect on Godly things such as wanting to be used by the Lord and fulfilling my God-given purpose, and as a result I began to seriously think about my commitment to the Lord. It did not take me long to realise that the Lord had been so faithful to me in my greatest time of need and that I had been wrong to withdraw from the assignment that He had given me. From that moment on, I determined in my heart that I would finish this book for the Lord.

It so happened that the summer break was coming up at school, so I made a decision to use this whole period to write the rest of this book. From May to July 2008, whenever anyone asked me what I would be doing during the summer break, I would confess, "I'm writing my book." I was not sure how I would cope with it all again, but I was certain that this time I would be handing all my cares over to the Lord to work them out on my behalf.

For the months leading up to the summer holiday, I constantly prayed about it and asked the Holy Spirit for His help in overcoming all the challenges that I had experienced the first time around, and I completely determined in my heart to have most of the book finished by the end of that summer holiday.

If you have ever determined in your heart to do something for the Lord which involves helping others and sharing the Gospel, you will probably know that the devil is not going to be happy about it and that he is going to use every weapon that he possibly can to prevent you from achieving your goals for God. I have known this reality for years, and I already knew that my co-operation with the Lord to write this book would upset the devil's kingdom. I wasn't blinded to this fact and I went into it with my eyes open. I was more than ready to stand up against the devil — or at least I thought I was!

The summer break came and I was all set to start writing this book again. The school holiday began on a Thursday, so I decided that I would have a couple of days of rest before dedicating myself to the book the following Monday. Everything seemed to be going fine and I was in great spirits about my task at hand.

On the Friday, I had a very upsetting feeling concerning my ex-partner. I don't know where it came from, but it was quite unpleasant for me. The feeling I was experiencing was upsetting because it was a fear that I had had for years, and to get a feeling like that so out of the blue worried me. The next day when I could not shake off this feeling, I decided to call him and share my feeling with him. To make a long story short, I came out and asked him, "Are you expecting another baby?" And to this he replied yes.

Now, after almost ten years of us being apart and me believing that I was completely over it all, you would have thought that such news would not have upset me, but the truth is that it did! I was absolutely devastated by his confirmation. For the next week, I could not think about anything other than this, and my plans to finish this book slowly began to loose their appeal.

After hearing this news, I began to experience a sick feeling in my stomach. Panic and fear began to set in, distressing thoughts started to bombard my mind. And just like I had experienced many years before, I started to go off my food and I was finding it hard to focus my attention on anything else.

Can you imagine how this all looked? I am about to write a book declaring how the Lord has completely healed me of my broken heart to help others and then I hear this news, which knocks me off my feet and forces me to ask myself the question, "But Lord, am I really healed?" I am not quite sure what you may be thinking at this moment, but for me I was thinking Lord maybe I'm not really healed after all and maybe I should not be the one writing this book for You. The whole situation seemed like a total nightmare!

However, after about a week of battling with my mind and flesh, with the help of the Holy Spirit I started to realise that this shocking news was a direct attack against me from the devil, and that his purpose was to distract me from finishing this book for the Lord.

I will not lie to you, this news really did upset and disappoint me, but at the same time, I determined to myself that I would not let it break me again. I had come so far on my journey from heartbreak and I was not going to give up on my destiny for anyone or anything. So with that in mind and the help of the Holy Spirit, I knew that at that moment I had two options. I could either succumb to the devil's tactics and let him win, or I could face the fire like Shadrach, Meshach, and Abednego in the book of Daniel, Chapter 3.

Not an easy choice, right? And I wish I could say that it was for me, but it wasn't. It took me about seven whole days to make up my mind about what I was going to do, but eventually *I chose to face the fire!*

In His presence!

"HE WHO dwells in the secret place of the Most High shall remain stable and fixed under the shadow of the Almighty [Whose power no foe can withstand]."

Psalms 91:1, AMP

I am not going to pretend that this part of my story was a straightforward process for me because it wasn't, but to make a long story short, I chose to run to the presence of the Lord! I made the decision that I was going to continue to write this book, as I had been directed to do by the Holy Spirit, and trust Him to help and protect me in my time of need.

In order for me to go through with my plans to write this book, I had to spend that whole summer immersed in the presence of the Lord. I would literally wake up every morning and ask the Holy Spirit to spend the day with me. From there, I would put on some soft praise and worship music in the background to block out all other interferences and stay in my room and share my thoughts, fear, challenges, confusion, pain, and joy with the Holy Spirit.

The peace that I experienced in His presence over this period was so heavenly that at times I did not want to leave it — even to visit the bathroom. It was awesome! I shared my heart with the Lord and in return He gave me the inspiration and power to let go of all my fears and the strength to write this book. Honestly, I would strongly recommend this course of action to anyone who is going through a difficult period. *Just get in His presence! (See Psalm 16:11).*

I am a worshipper and I love to worship the Lord. My constant prayer and heart's desire is to worship the Lord God in spirit and in truth *(see John 4:23-24)*, and I especially like to worship the Lord in song and through music. During this time in the presence of the Lord, I experienced a very strong urge to worship Him like never before — so I did. I used this time of worship to block out all the attempts of the devil to distract me from my task and it worked. My focus shifted from me and all that was going on around me to the Lord and fulfilling His assignment for my life.

One morning during the summer holiday, as I was worshipping the Lord, I began to sense in my spirit that something was missing from me. I sensed that a piece of my heart was missing. I am not silly, and straight away I knew why I was feeling like this. It was because a part of my heart was still with my ex-partner and until now, I had been happy for it to stay there. However, when I began to think about and reflect upon all the unnecessary pain that it was still causing me, I decided there and then that it was time for me to take it back. I made a decision that I no longer wanted this person to have a piece of my heart anymore! At this, I sat on the edge of my bed and cried out to the Lord, "Please give me back my heart! Lord, I just want my complete heart back! Please restore my heart and soul!"

On that morning, I can honestly say that when I made that plea to the Lord to give me back my heart I really meant every word of that prayer!

Everyone will experience a defining moment at some point or another in their lives, a moment where they will have to make a very important decision, and I guess that day was mine!

I spent the rest of the day in a state of worship. I spent my day loving the Lord, thanking Him for everything He had done for me, and singing His praises. It was a very peaceful day!

When evening came, I got myself ready to go to a prayer meeting at church. I went that evening not expecting anything. I just wanted to continue to worship my Lord with all my heart and give Him thanks and praise because I love Him.

The moment I walked into church, I could sense that the presence of God was there and I was quite excited about this. There were quite a few people there praying and the atmosphere was perfect. We all prayed for awhile and then Pastor Clem announced that he was going to anoint each of us with oil before the meeting ended.

As I walked forward to Pastor Clem for prayer the presence of God became so heavy upon me that I started to weep. These tears were not of sadness or pain, they were an expression of my gratitude towards the Lord for who He is and what He had done for me. At that point Pastor Clem laid his hands on my forehead and began to pray for me, "Lord, restore her heart and soul! Restore it completely! Everything trying to hinder her breakthrough in this area, I come against you with the blood of Jesus! Let her heart and soul be restored today in Jesus' Name!"

Wow. At first I was a little taken aback by the words Pastor Clem was praying over me because I couldn't believe that he was praying a similar prayer request to the one I had prayed for myself earlier that morning. I had not shared my conversation with the Lord that morning with anyone, so when Pastor began to minister to me in this way I knew instantly that the Lord was answering my prayer request and restoring my heart and soul back to me.

Pastor Clem spent awhile ministering to me, and while he was doing so I actually felt like something was being restored within me.

I left church that night in total amazement. When I had asked the Lord to restore my soul and give me back my heart that morning, I had not expected Him to act so quickly but He did, and it was amazing!

"And it shall come to pass in that day, that his burden shall be taken away from off thy shoulder, and his yoke from off thy neck, and the yoke shall be destroyed because of the anointing."

Isaiah 10:2, KJV

A couple of weeks after this prayer meeting, I began to notice that whenever I heard or thought about something concerning my ex-partner, I did not respond or react to it in the same way that I had done before. I no longer felt tied to him. It was like the connection I had with him had been removed from me and I was free. It was a weird feeling and a bit strange to begin with, but for the first time in years I felt emotionally free from my ex-partner. It was at this point that I actually knew that the Lord had restored my soul and had given me back my whole heart!

Have faith!

"And Jesus, replying, said to them, Have faith in God [constantly]. Truly I tell you, whoever says to this mountain, Be lifted up and thrown into the sea! and does not doubt at all in his heart but believes that what he says will take place, it will be done for him. For this reason I am telling you, whatever you ask for in prayer, believe (trust and be confident) that it is granted to you, and you will [get it]."

Mark 11:22-24, AMP

I'm going to honest with you; it takes a lot to have faith in God! It isn't easy! I used to read Mark 11:23-24 and think to myself, "Is Jesus really serious? How on earth can you say to a mountain 'Be lifted and thrown into the sea,' and expect it to actually happen?" This concept was way beyond me! In fact, to begin with, it was Scriptures like these that made it quite difficult for me to trust God and take Him at His

Word. To the natural mind it is impossible, but with God nothing is impossible *(Luke 1:37)*.

I struggled with the whole idea of trusting the Lord with real life issues for years, and it was only after I made a decision to put my complete trust in God and put His Word to the test that He was able to prove to me that He is totally reliable and able to meet all my needs.

In closing, I would like to strongly encourage you all to have faith in God because *"Without faith it is impossible to please him: for he that cometh to God must believe that he is, and that he is a rewarder of them that diligently seek him"* (Hebrews 11:6 KJV).

Whatever your situation may be, if you really want to get through it and over to the other side *you will have to have faith in God!*

The End!

Throughout this book I have openly and honestly shared my testimony with you. I have shared my heart, my pain, my triumphs, my insight and of course my victories. I have prayed for you and with you, and I have also shared the wisdom the Holy Spirit has shared with me.

I hope that my story has been more than just a story to you. I hope that it has ministered to your heart and soul, inspired you, and that it has given you the strength and courage that you need to overcome your own struggles.

If this book has truly blessed and helped you I am eternally grateful to the Lord God Almighty for helping and using me to accomplish this great task.

Before I close this book there is one last thing that I want to ask of you: when the Lord heals your broken heart and gives you the freedom that you long for, please go and share your own testimony with others!

And finally, as the year 2008 gets ready to close and we get ready to enter into the year 2009 — 'The Year of Progression and Positive Change', I wish to declare to the world: **"It is finished!"**

"Closing Prayer"

I love You, I love You, I love You!

My heavenly Father, the Most High God, I can remember back in 2007 when I first wrote my Opening Prayer. It seems like such a long time ago, but when I wrote it I already knew then that I could not get through this task without You. So I decided to take the step of faith and thank You in advance — and it paid off!

Since then the journey that You have taken me on has been unbelievable. I cannot believe that I have come this far in such a short space of time. Your grace and mercy have definitely brought me through!

Daddy, I thank You for believing in me at a time when I could not see the potential that You placed inside of me (Jeremiah 1:5). I thank You for putting this book into my heart and giving me this opportunity to become a vessel for Your use. It is a complete honour and I don't take it lightly. I also want to thank You for coming into my life and being the Father that my heart and soul so desperately longed for. And I thank You for the unconditional love that You have lavished on me —You truly are my *Father*!

"I will lift up mine eyes unto the hills, from whence cometh my help. My help cometh from the LORD, which made heaven and earth. You will not suffer my foot to be moved: You that keepeth me will not slumber. Behold, You that keepeth Israel shall neither slumber nor sleep. The LORD is my keeper: the LORD is my shade upon my right hand. The sun shall not smite me by day, nor the moon by night. The LORD shall preserve me from all evil: You shall preserve my soul. The LORD shall preserve my going out and my coming in from this time forth, and even for evermore."

Psalm 121 KJV, (personalisation added)

My Heavenly Father, let Your will be done on this earth, as it is in heaven. And let Your Kingdom come!

Printed in the United Kingdom by
Lightning Source UK Ltd., Milton Keynes
141893UK00002B/16/P